Never Never Lands

Western Australian Outback

To chronicle the creation stories of the city, Unknown Fields head off on a dust-blown road trip across Australia, into the vast and mysterious interior of this remote island continent in search of its ancient tribal hinterlands and its immense techno-landscapes. Beneath the Southern Cross, machines harvest the earth for the precious ingredients of our daily lives. We stalk mechanical beasts the size of buildings and explore excavations the size of cities. Here, in the Never Never, are the resource territories of the city, a land of rich geology, endless horizons and mining pits so large that they generate their own weather systems. Towering mountains of tailings, remade landforms, terraced valleys and artificial lakes all take shape from this distributed ground. Violent gestures of accelerated geology create landscapes of erasure, excavation and re-articulation.

    For this book, Unknown Fields travel 1km beneath the surface of the earth in search of gold, to survey and laser-scan the technological incisions that release it from the ground. We follow tunnels winding below Australia's red crust and stand at the base of the mega pits that are cut through the narrative landscape of the Dreamtime, the creation mythology of the Aboriginal Australians. Stories and ceremonies of dreaming beings that once formed the sacred sites of mountain ranges and river-beds are now spun with the ghosts of modern technologies, family heirlooms and financial fictions. Territories once mapped into surfaces of Aboriginal dot paintings are now depicted on screen in the digital point clouds of geology survey scans. Stories from two indigenous authors act as our Dreamtime guide as we drift across the grounds of traditional creation, before diving deep to follow a new subterranean songline, one created from underground mine computer models and laser survey data. We retrace a constellation of gold artefacts scattered across the earth back through mine pits and tunnels to their origin in ore bodies deep below. Roughly 0.034grams of this landscape is locked away in each of our mobile phones, charged and quietly vibrating. We all carry a little piece of Australia in our pockets.

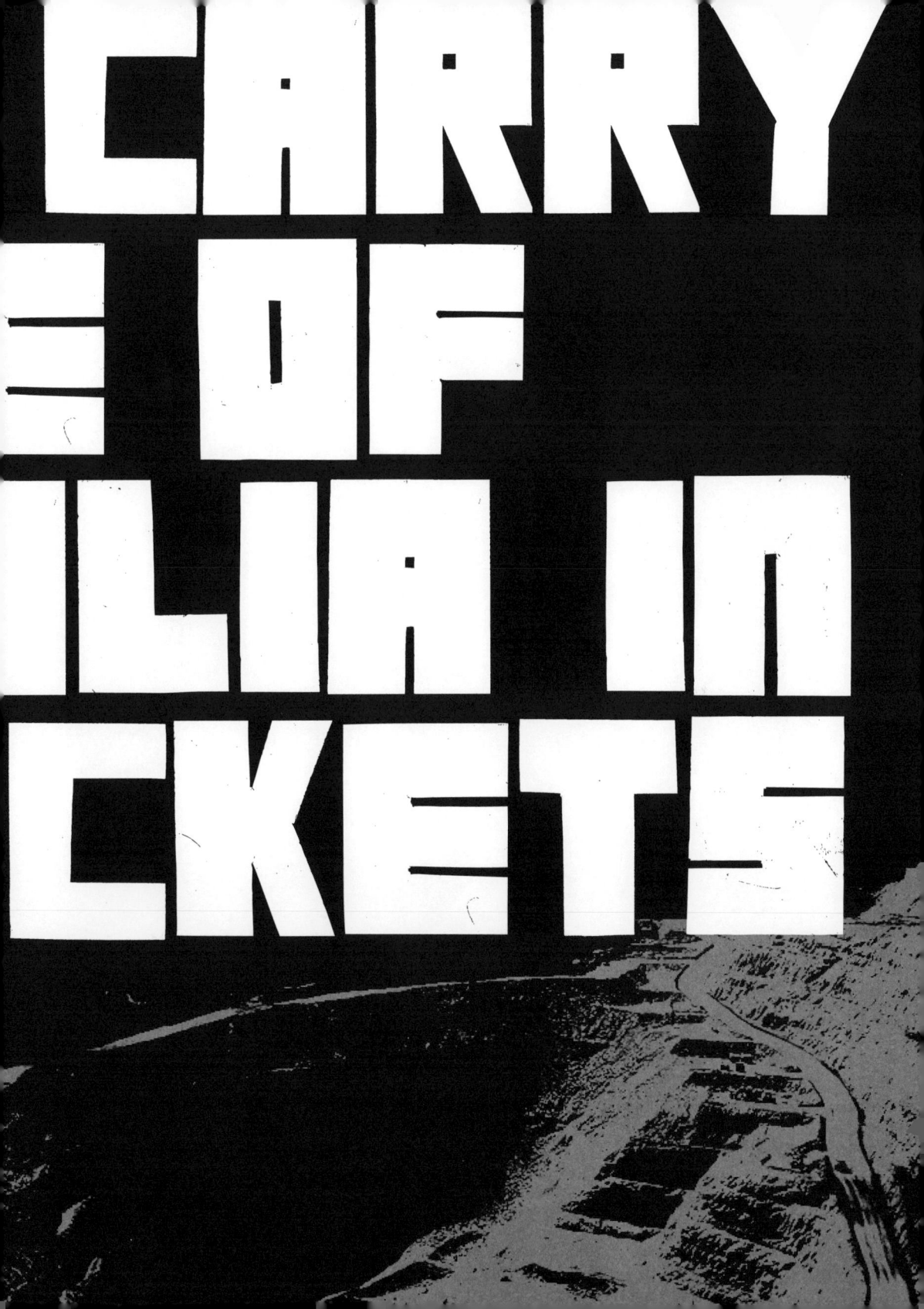

Distributed Ground

Our city of gold casts a long shadow across the earth. Here lies the silent twin: the void where a landform once was. An ancient landscape scattered and redistributed, remade into bullion in a vault, a grandmother's ring, a gangster's tooth, electrical connections, a gold-plated revolver, a haul of Roman coins in a museum or gold flakes in a shot glass. From the ground comes a catalogue of gold objects. Every object leaves a trace and the fluctuations of the gold price on the market sends ripples through the earth. The territories of Australia become atomised into a constellation of glistening things scattered around the world. The dust of Australia blows gold.

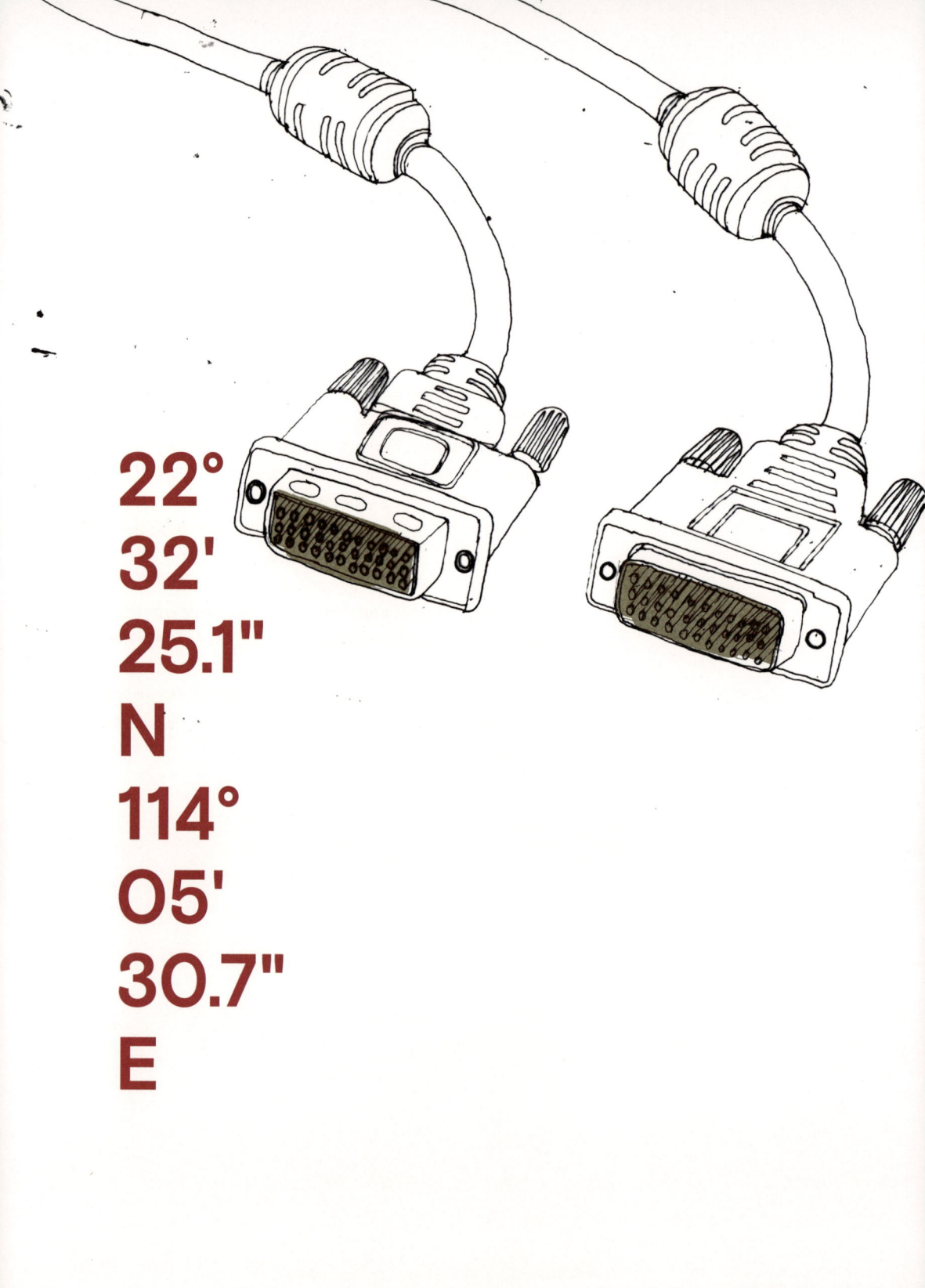

22° 43' 59.1" N 114° 13' 01.9" E

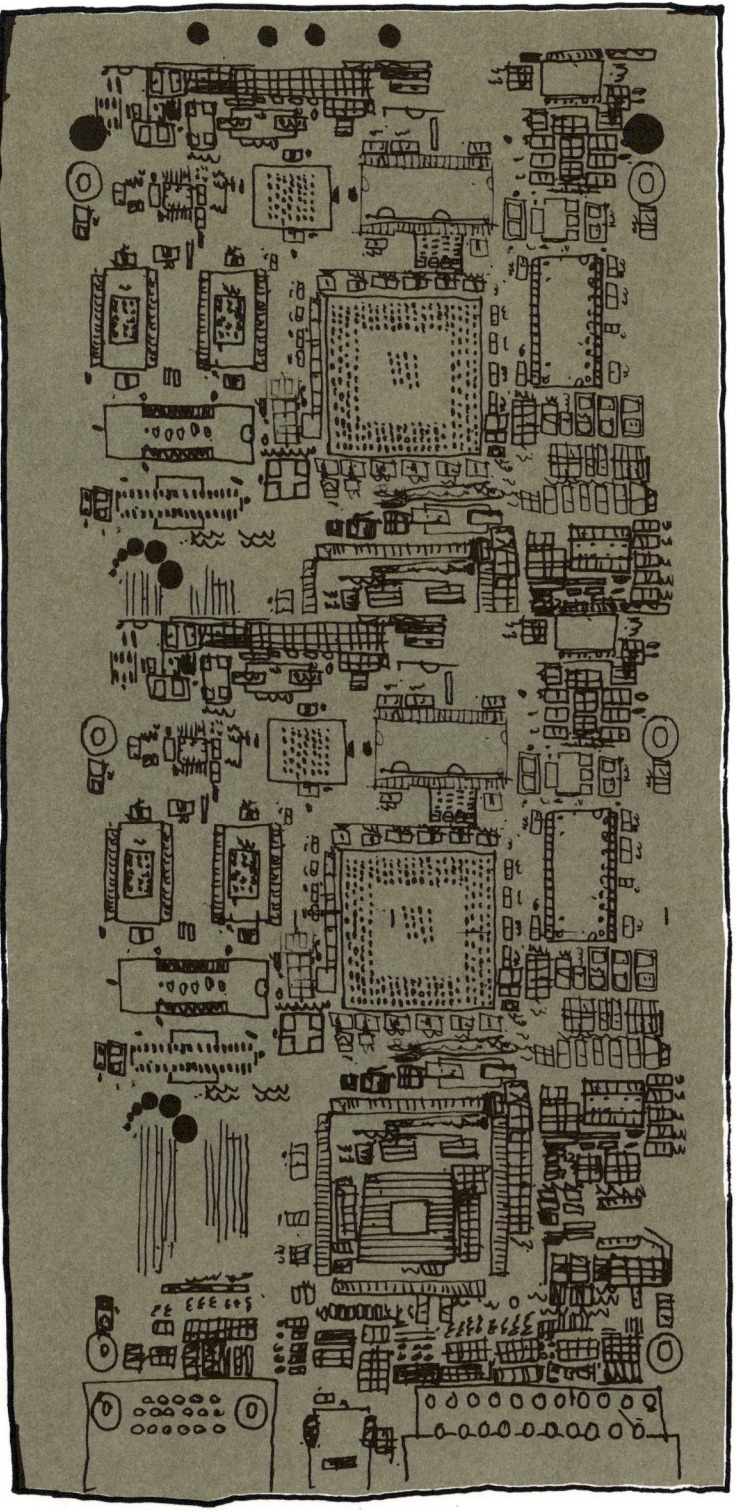

30°
47'
3.00"
S
121°
30'
30.25"
E

33° 53' 32.6" N 118° 13' 54.4 W

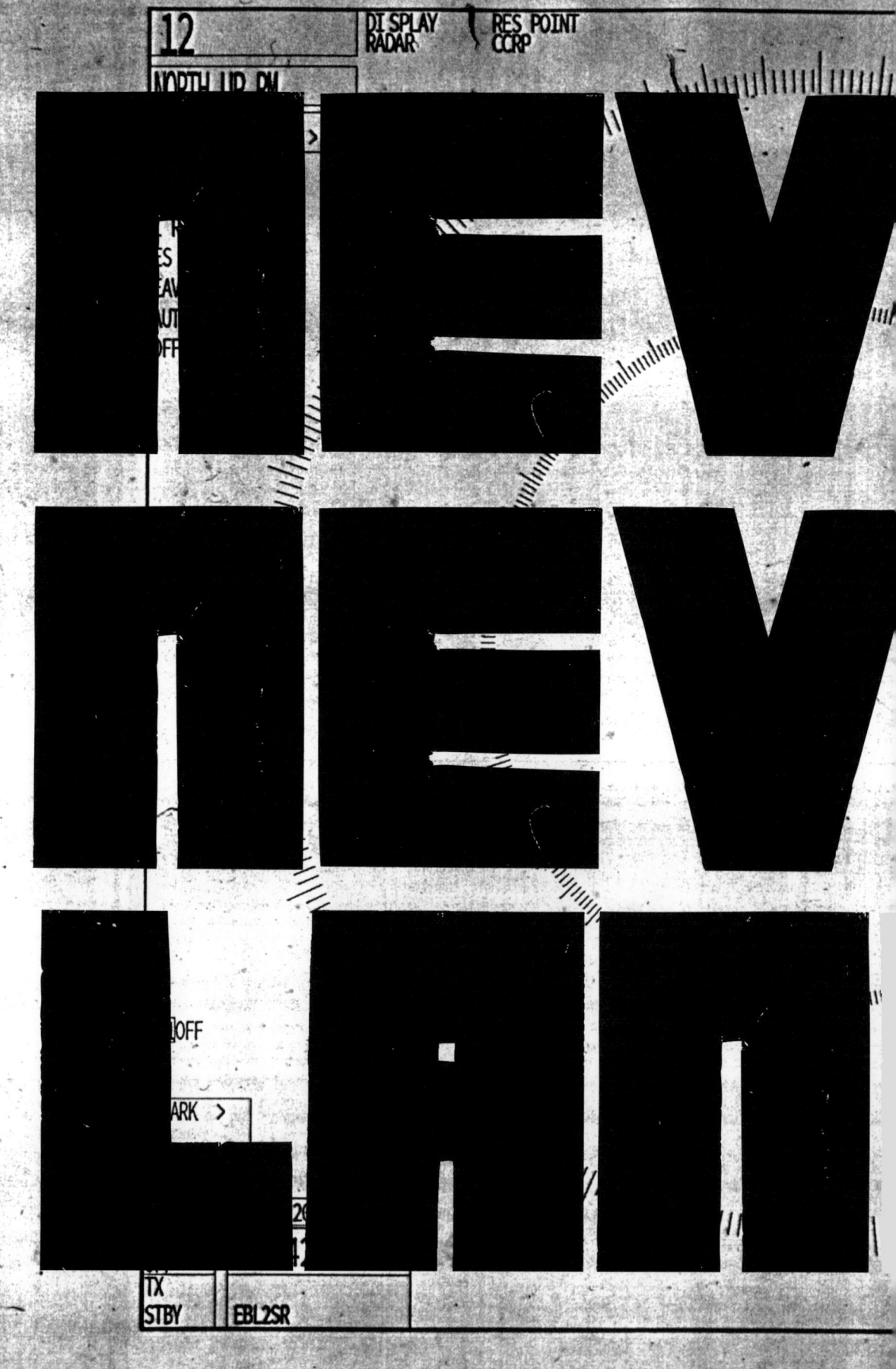

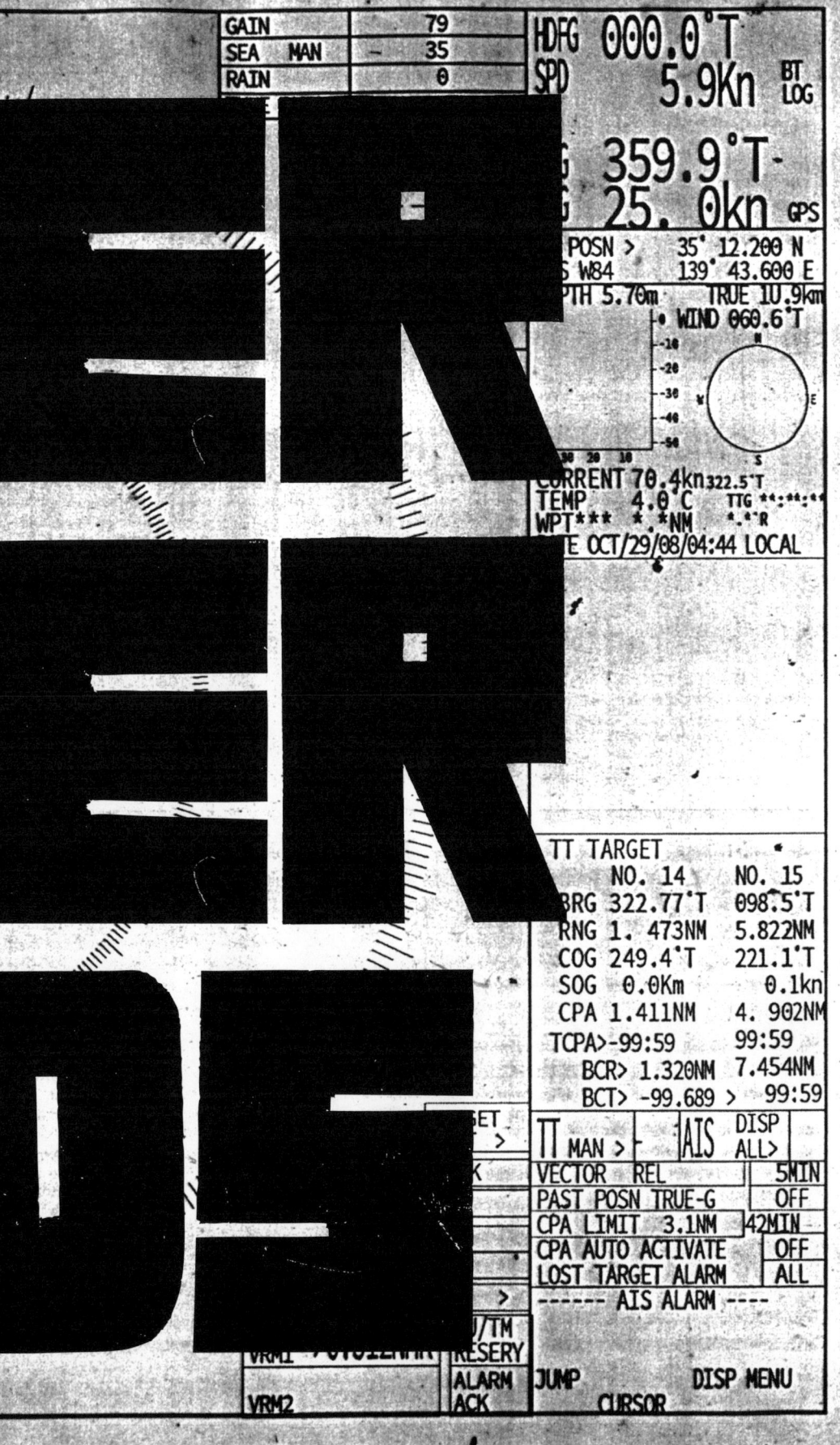

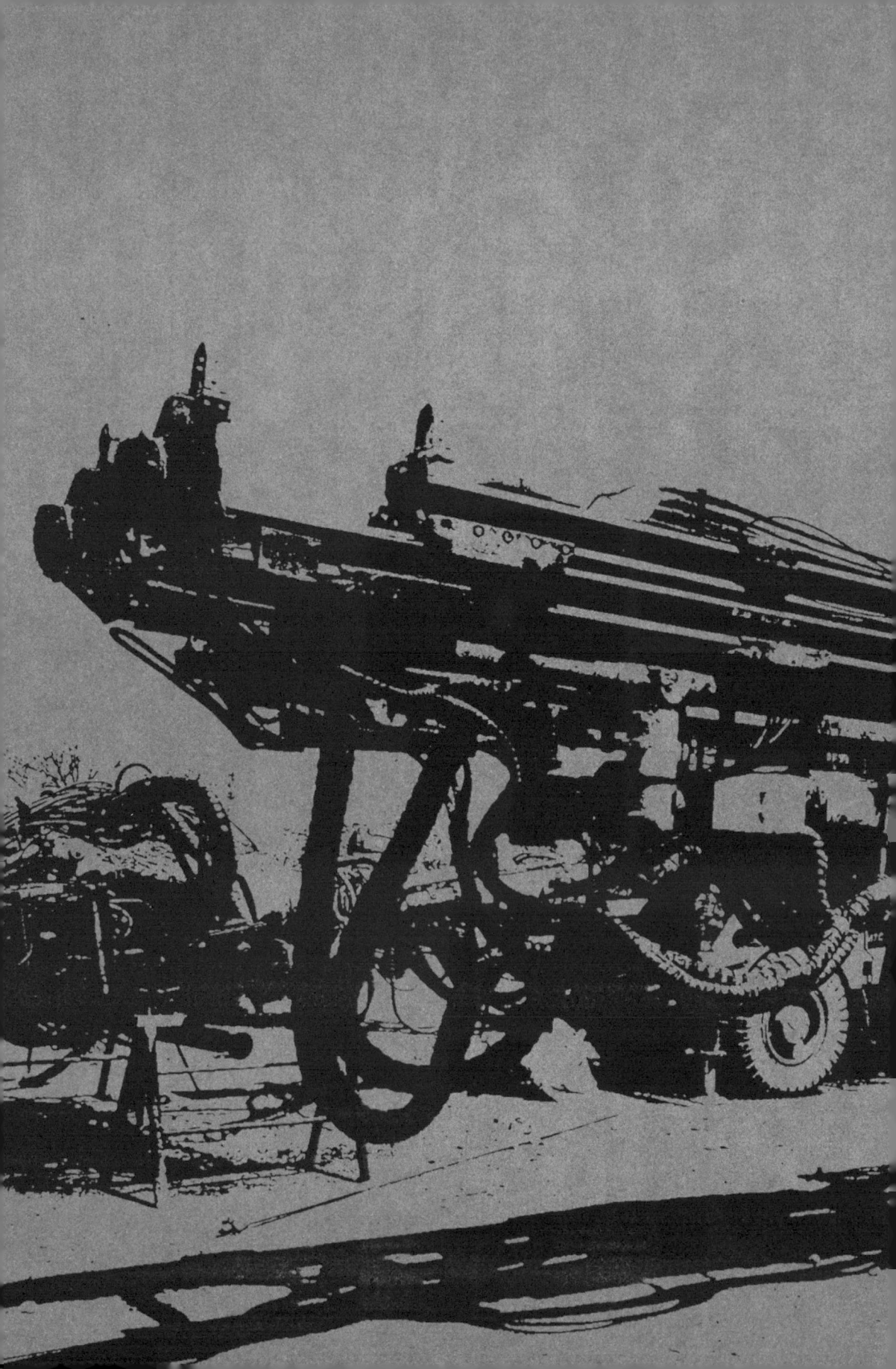

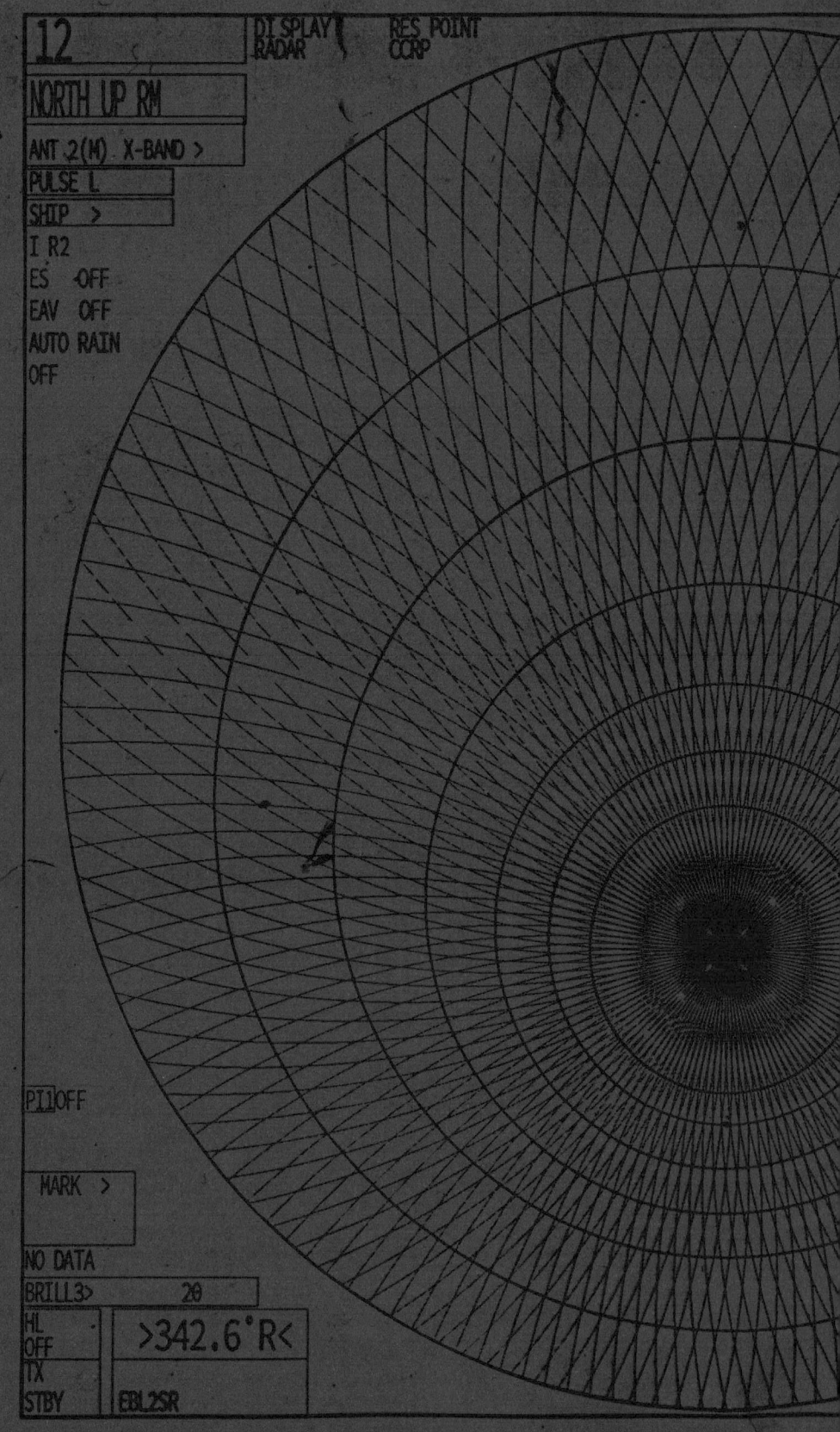

When the Earth Was Soft

Words by Indigenous Australian author
Alexis Wright. An extract from *Carpentaria*,
Giramondo, 2006.

From time immemorial

NATION CHANTS, BUT WE KNOW YOUR STORY ALREADY.
THE BELLS PEAL EVERYWHERE. CHURCH BELLS CALLING
THE FAITHFUL TO THE TABERNACLE WHERE THE GATES
OF HEAVEN WILL OPEN, BUT NOT FOR THE WICKED.
CALLING INNOCENT LITTLE BLACK GIRLS FROM A DISTANT
ABORIGINAL COMMUNITY WHERE THE WHITE DOVE BEARING
AN OLIVE BRANCH NEVER LANDS. LITTLE GIRLS WHO COME
BACK HOME AFTER CHURCH ON SUNDAY, WHO LOOK AROUND
THEMSELVES AT THE HUMAN FALLOUT AND ANNOUNCE
MATTER-OF-FACTLY, ARMAGEDDON BEGINS HERE.

The ancestral serpent, a creature larger than
storm clouds, came down from the stars, laden
with its own creative enormity. It moved
graciously – if you had been watching with the
eyes of a bird hovering in the sky far above
the ground. Looking down at the serpent's wet
body, glistening from the ancient sunlight,
long before man was a creature who could
contemplate the next moment in time. It came
down those billions of years ago, to crawl on
its heavy belly, all around the wet clay soils
in the Gulf of Carpentaria.
    Picture the creative serpent, scoring
deep into – scouring down through – the slippery
underground of the mudflats, leaving in its wake
the thunder of tunnels collapsing to form deep
sunken valleys. The sea water following in the
serpent's wake, swarming in a frenzy of tidal
waves, soon changed colour from ocean blue to

the yellow of mud. The water filled the swirling tracks to form the mighty bending rivers spread across the vast plains of the gulf country. The serpent travelled over the marine plains, over the salt flats, through the salt dunes, past the mangrove forests and crawled inland. Then it went back to the sea. And it came out at another spot along the coastline and crawled inland and back again. When it finished creating the many rivers in its wake, it created one last river, no larger or smaller than the others, a river which offers no apologies for its discontent with people who do not know it. This is where the giant serpent continues to live deep down under the ground in a vast network of limestone aquifers. They say its being is porous; it permeates everything. It is all around in the atmosphere and is attached to the lives of the river people like skin.

This tidal river snake of flowing mud takes in breaths of a size that is difficult to comprehend. Imagine the serpent's breathing rhythms as the tide flows inland, edging towards the spring waters nestled deeply in the gorges of an ancient limestone plateau covered with rattling grasses dried yellow from the prevailing winds. Then with the outward breath, the tide turns and the serpent flows back to its own circulating mass of shallow waters in the giant water basin in a crook of the mainland whose sides separate it from the open sea.

To catch this breath in the river you need the patience of one who can spend days doing nothing. If you wait under the rivergum where those up-to-no-good mission-bred kids accidentally hanged Cry-baby Sally, the tip of the dead branch points to where you will see how the serpent's breath fights its way through

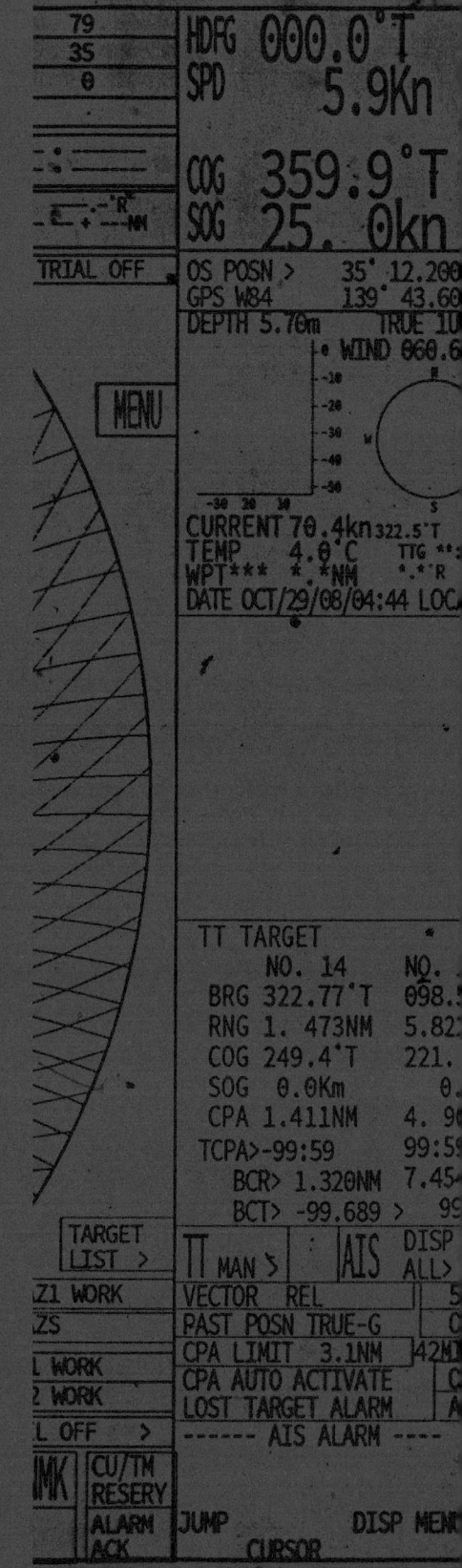

in a tunnel of wind, creating ripples that shimmer silver, similar to the scales of a small, nocturnal serpent, thrashing in anger whenever the light hits its slippery translucent body, making it writhe and wrench to escape back into its natural environment of darkness.

The inside knowledge about this river and coastal region is the Aboriginal Law handed down through the ages since time began. Otherwise, how would one know where to look for the hidden underwater courses in the vast flooding mud plains, full of serpents and fish in the monsoon season? Can someone who did not grow up in a place that is sometimes under water, sometimes bone-dry, know when the trade winds blowing off the southern and northern hemispheres will merge in summer? Know the moment of climatic change better than they know themselves? Who fishes in the yellow-coloured monsoonal runoff from the drainages, with sheets of deep water pouring into the wide rivers swollen over their banks, filling vast plains with floodwaters? The cyclones linger and regroup, the rain never stops pouring, but the fat fish are abundant.

It takes a particular kind of knowledge to go with the river, whatever its mood. It is about there being no difference between you and the movement of water as it seasonally shifts its tracks according to its own mood. A river that spurns human endeavour in one dramatic gesture, jilting a lover who has never really been known, as it did to the frontier town built on its banks in the hectic heyday of colonial vigour. A town intended to serve as a port for the shipping trade for the hinterland of Northern Australia.

AW

Subterranean Dreaming

Forged from the ancient supercontinent of Ur, the ground of Western Australia is formed from some of the oldest rocks on the planet. Aboriginal dreamtime narratives speak of a time when the ground was soft and creation beings shaped mountains and rivers. When the rainbow serpent slinked across the ground to create a river, and a wild dog came to rest to form a mountain. Now as the lights of the city wash out the sky the songlines walked by these ancestral spirits are sung anew with the tracks laid down by the beasts of the mining industry. Here, as explosives, diggers and drills replace the slow erosion of rivers and winds, new stories are being told.

    The dreaming landscape that embodies the creation stories of Aboriginal Australians is overlaid with a vast infrastructure of resource speculation and financial fictions. Geological survey planes track back and forth, laser-scanning the earth searching for the topographic anomalies that indicate pockets of undiscovered minerals in the ground. The millions of points created by their scans are examined to determine territories for core sampling. These in turn give form to subterranean outcrops, features and landmarks, bands and shards of material riches under the dry red dirt.

    Aboriginal native title rights apply to the surface of the earth but exclude the valuable subsurface minerals which all belong to the state. No one is yet singing the creation stories of the ore body formations below ground. They are voids in waiting, fragments of a country destined to be taken away ship by ship.

Traditional dot paintings of dreamtime stories have often been used to support land rights claims but now the dots of the point cloud data force a different type of claim on the landscape. The technologies with which this ground is surveyed, depicted and recorded also become the means through which we claim ownership over it. Constructed from 3D laser scans, underground mine models and aerial survey data, these point-cloud paintings, take us on a subterranean journey — a worm's eye view of the ore bodies, open-pits and tunnel excavations of the gold mines of Western Australia. The images recontextualise the data from economic assessments of these landscapes within the narrative of an alternative cultural reading.

Underneath our feet lies an inverted landscape of glistening mineral-laden earth and dormant nuggets destined to take the form of the city's desires. This is a story about a material valued above all others, but there exists a parallel story, about the value of this landscape untouched.

26° 37' 57.79" S 120° 15' 10.25" E

Ochre is the Dried Up Blood of Ancient Creatures.

Words by Indigenous Australian author Tyson Mowarin

In the long darkness, the cold wind blows across the mountain peaks, strong and wild, showing no mercy for what lies in its path. This new landscape is born. The very first light shines on the high peaks; young, wild and free but still soft… for this is the beginning of time.

'Thunderous roars of boulders falling and moving across the landscape preparing to find their final resting place, the earth shook, rumbled and groaned while the landscapes were formed…, this is the time of creation.'

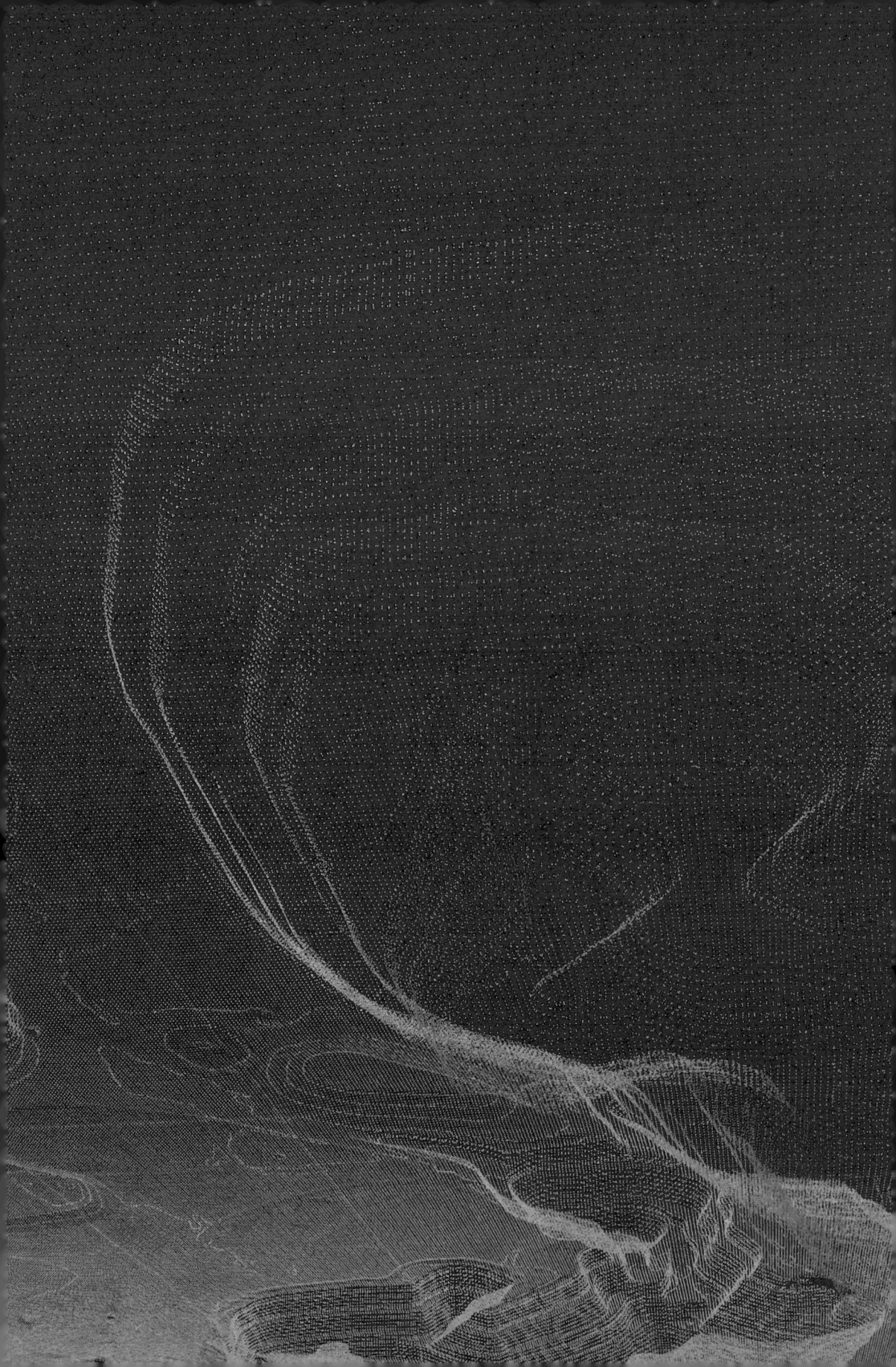

'The land has a living spirit, she hears, she sees, she feels. The spirit of the land has always been alive. She hears you when you are out enjoying her presence and She also hears the silence when you are not. She sees you and enjoys your beauty and she feels when you care for her, she feels pain when you hurt her and is lonely when she is by herself.'

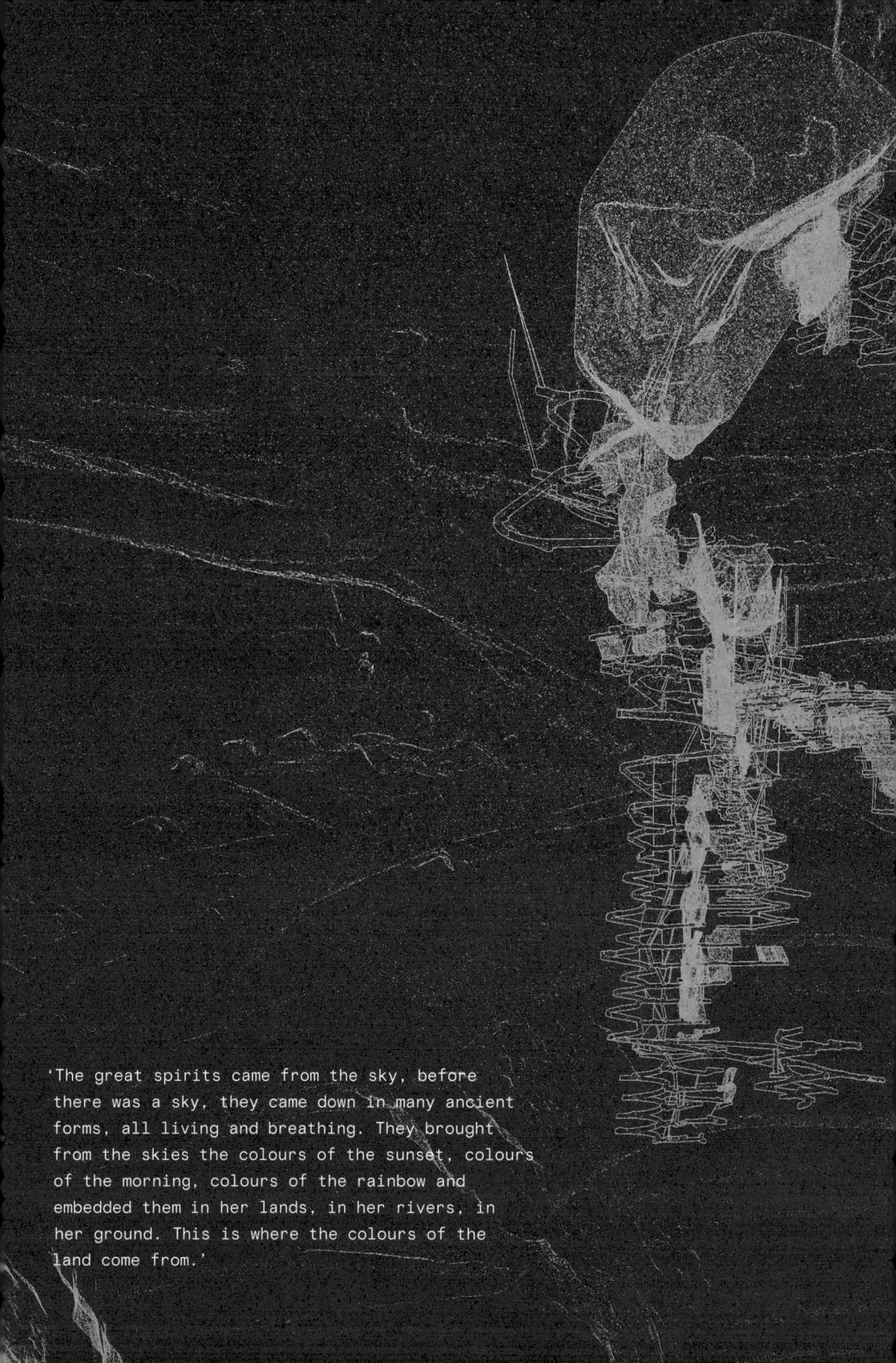

'The great spirits came from the sky, before there was a sky, they came down in many ancient forms, all living and breathing. They brought from the skies the colours of the sunset, colours of the morning, colours of the rainbow and embedded them in her lands, in her rivers, in her ground. This is where the colours of the land come from.'

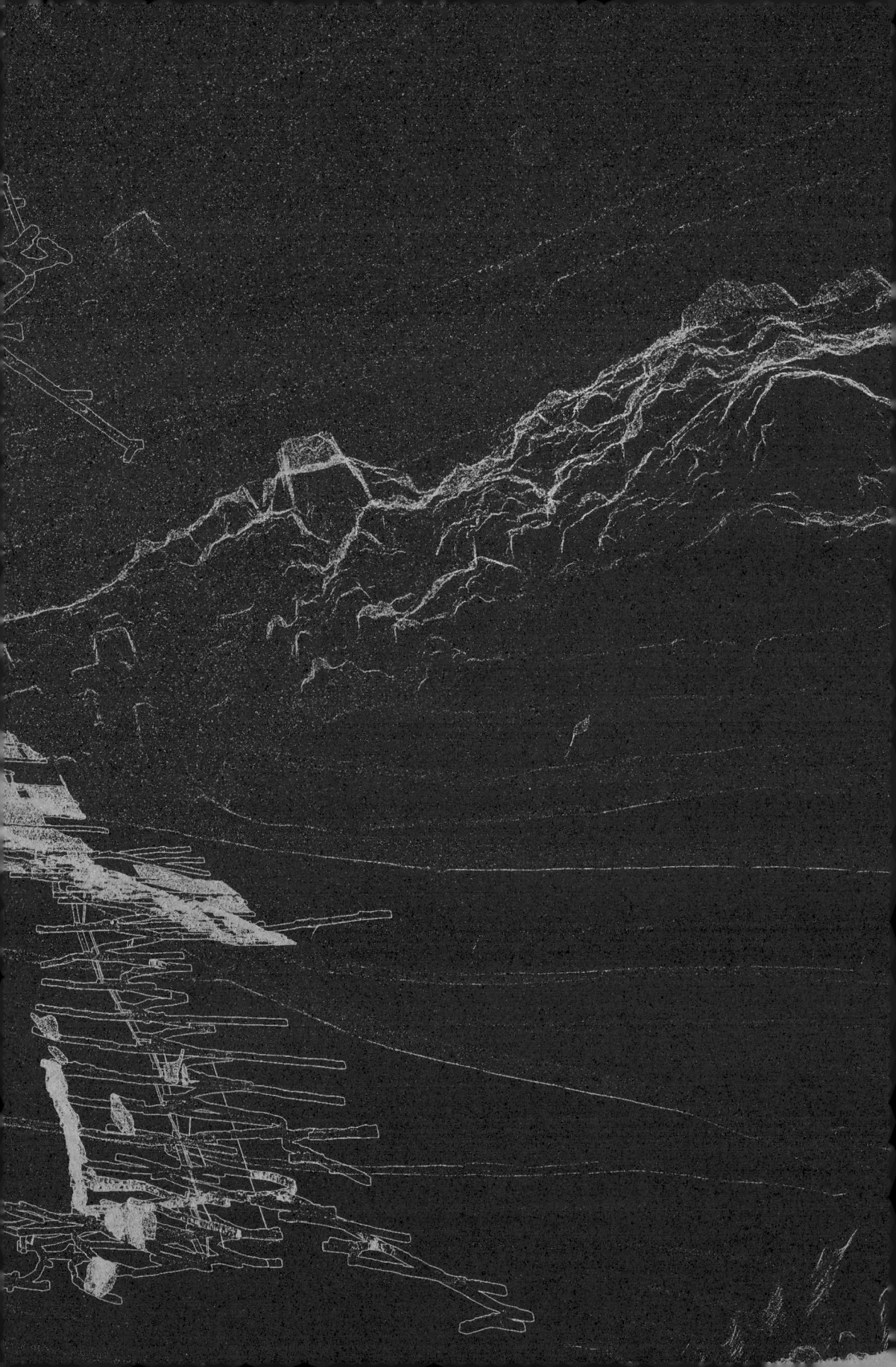

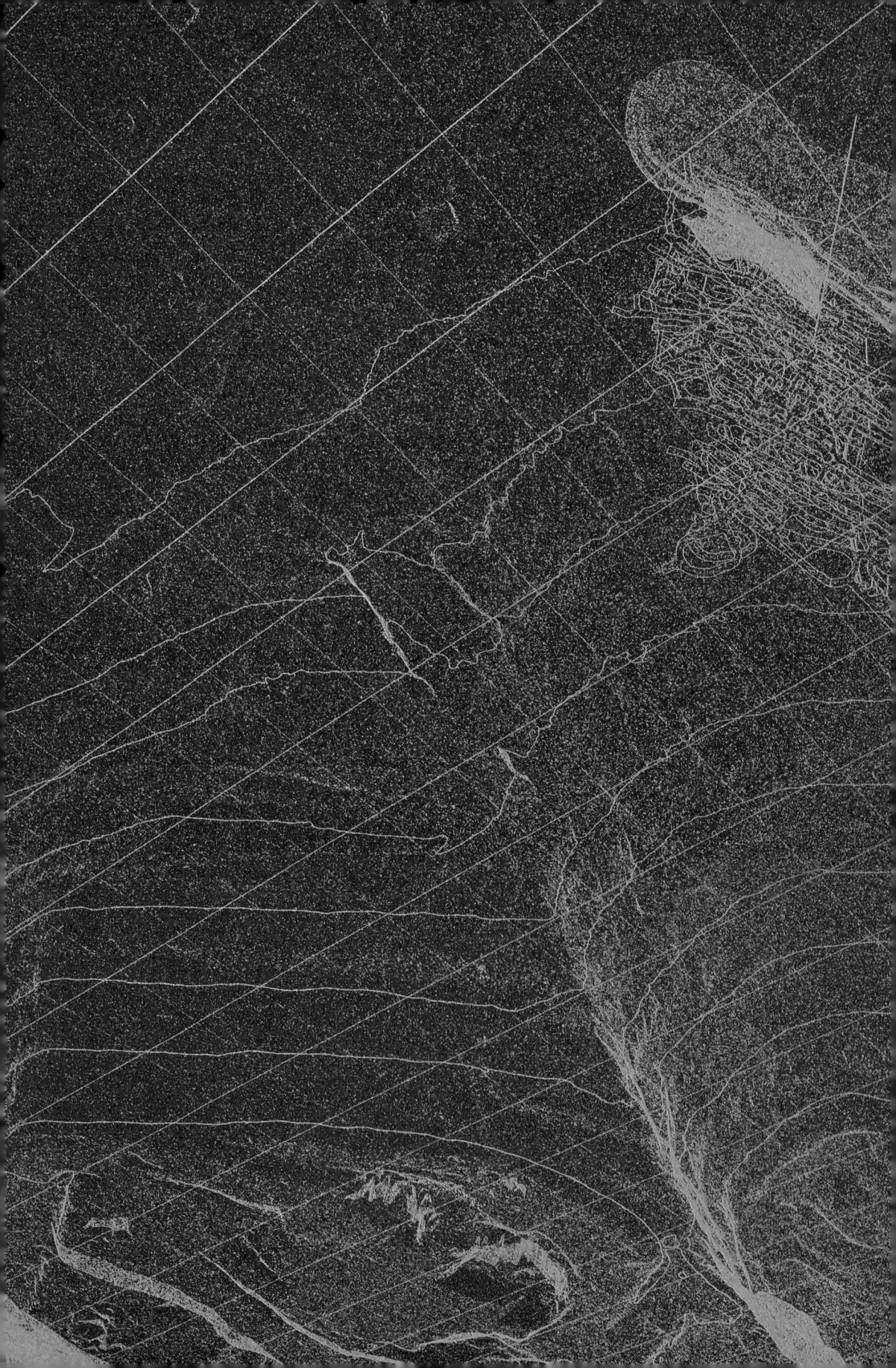

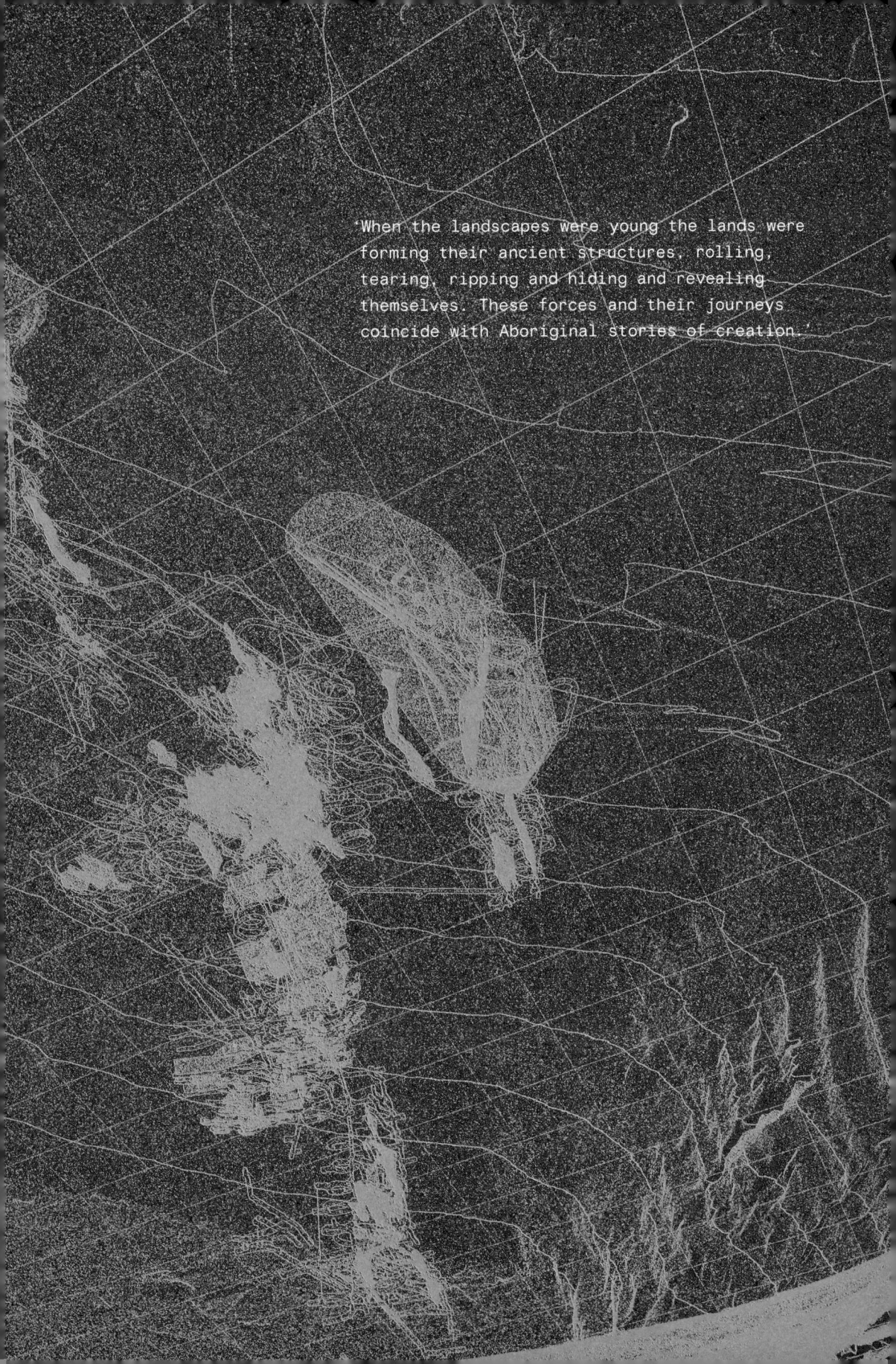

'Right across our ancient lands, from the sand islands and Great Barrier Reef in the east to the ancient landscapes that form the Murujuga or Burrup Peninsula in the west of Australia, where the world's biggest and most comprehensive petroglyph rock art gallery lives, the stories of creation times are eerily accurate and reflect what we see in the land today.'

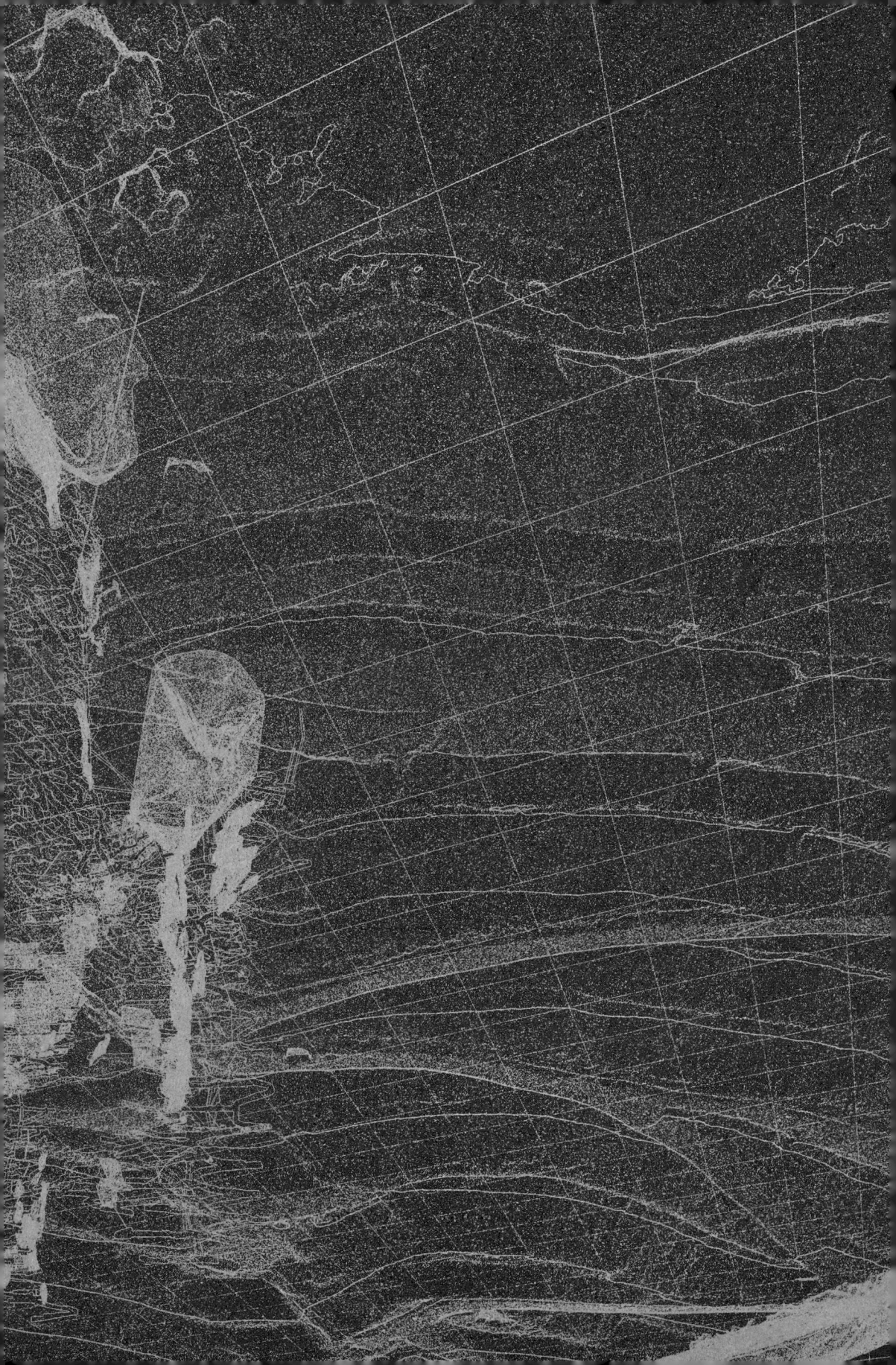

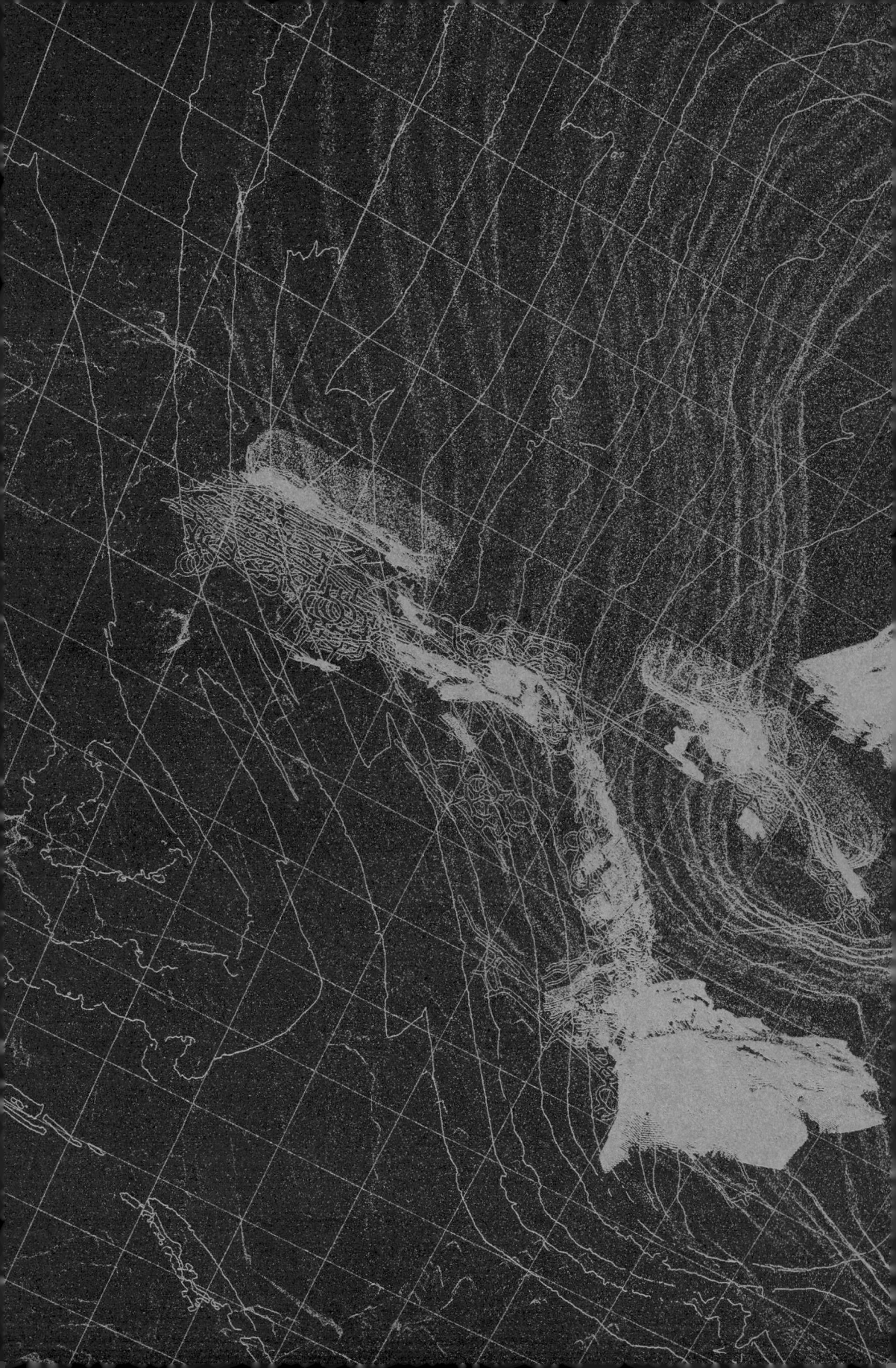

'There are stories of fierce battles, man vs man and spirit vs man and ancient creation gods that fought an almost mythical monster, slaying each other and leaving huge deposits of blood that turned into our blood-red ochre, or the charcoal remains of an ancient animal or forest that turned into coal and eventually diamonds. The tears of a sky god that flooded ancient landscapes, forming the places we see today.'

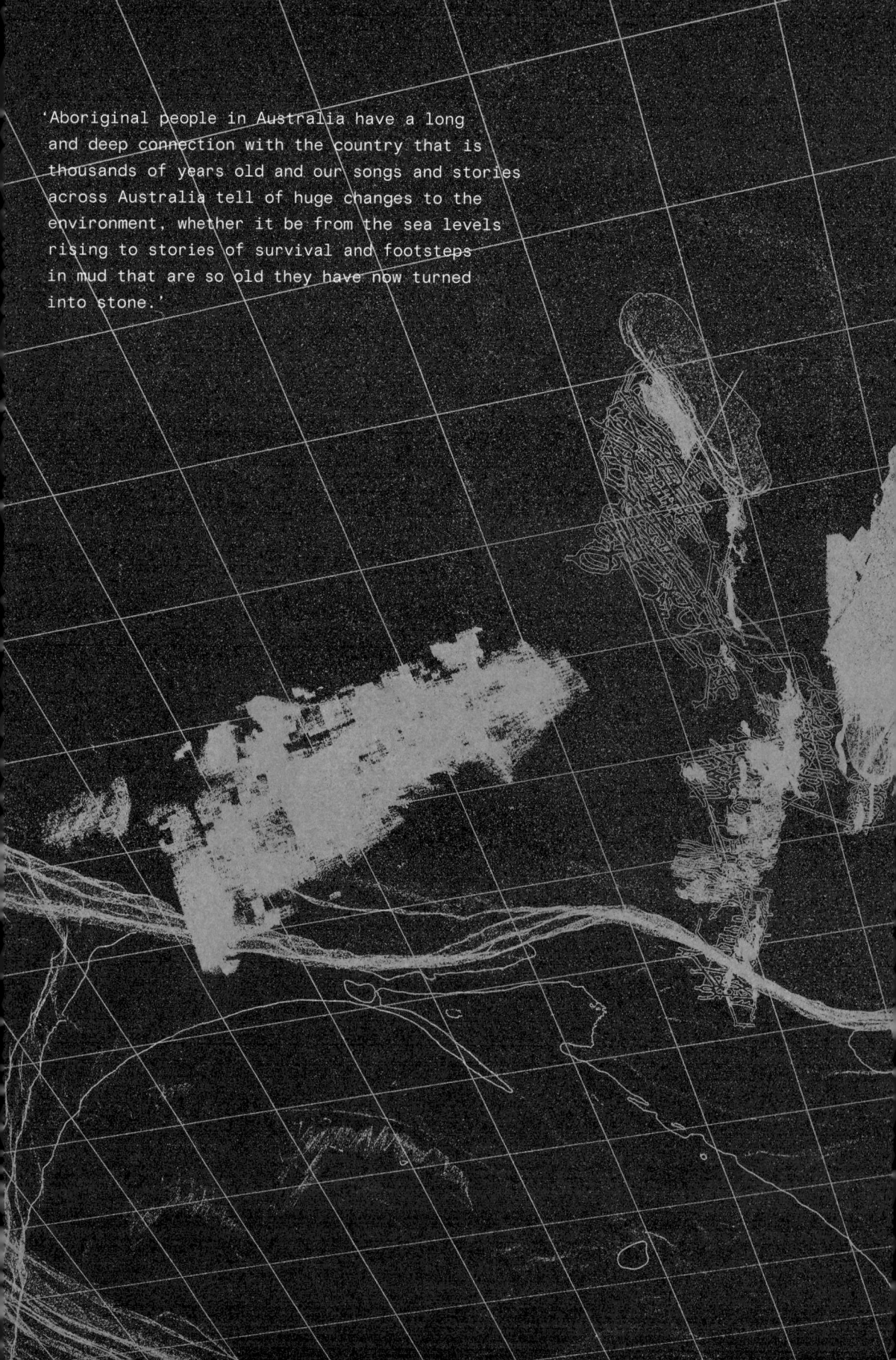

'Aboriginal people in Australia have a long and deep connection with the country that is thousands of years old and our songs and stories across Australia tell of huge changes to the environment, whether it be from the sea levels rising to stories of survival and footsteps in mud that are so old they have now turned into stone.'

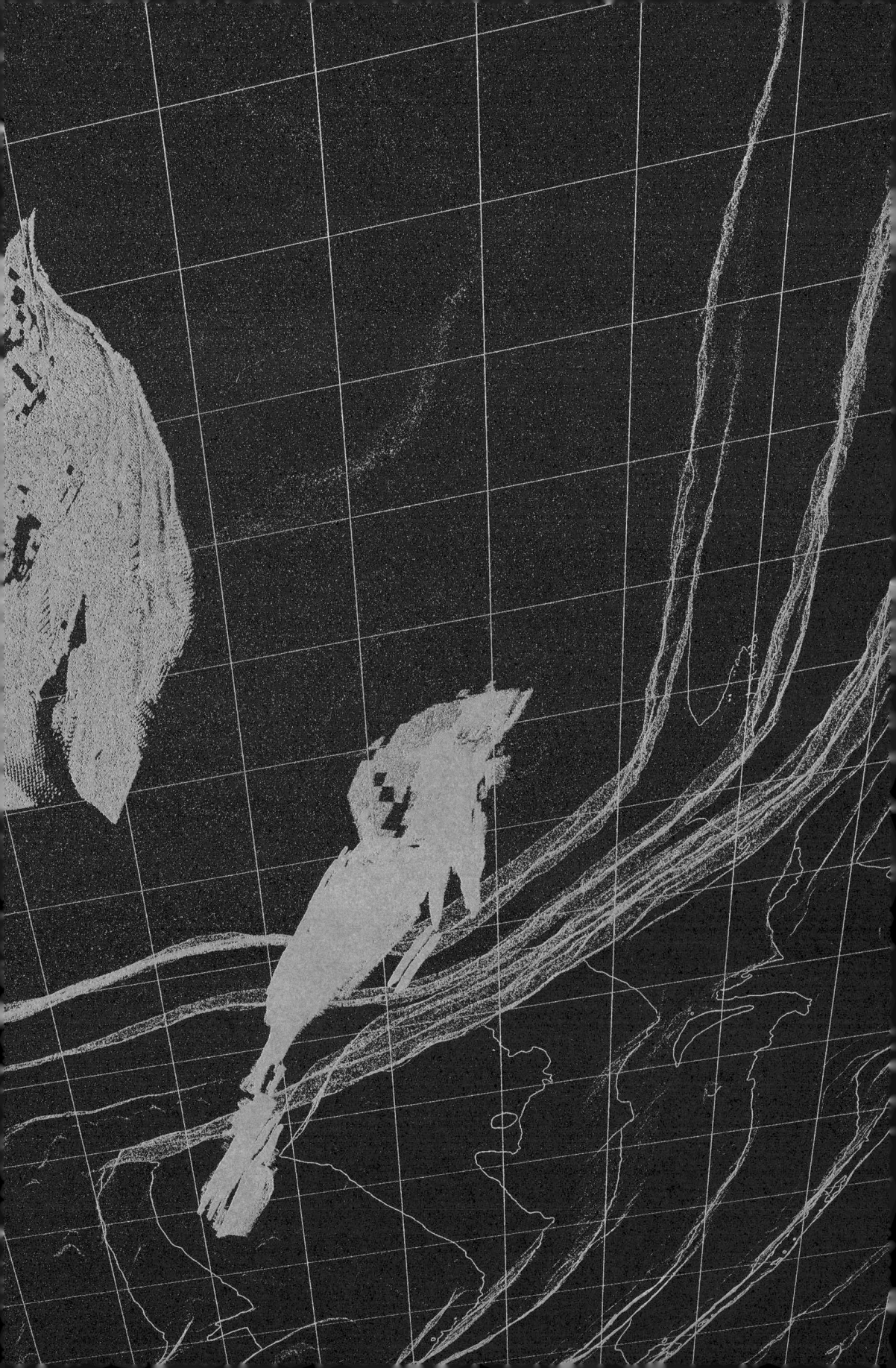

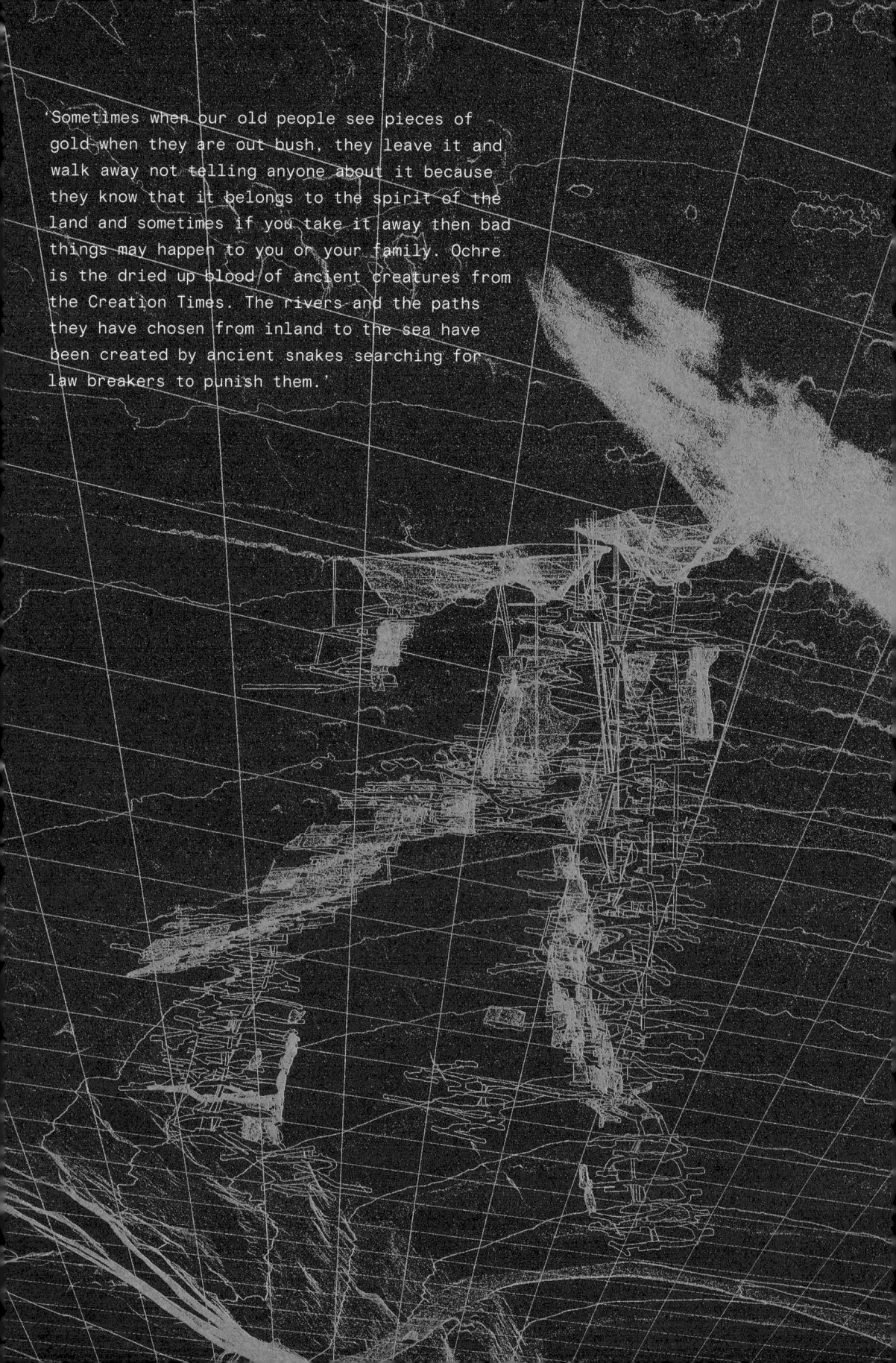

'Sometimes when our old people see pieces of gold when they are out bush, they leave it and walk away not telling anyone about it because they know that it belongs to the spirit of the land and sometimes if you take it away then bad things may happen to you or your family. Ochre is the dried up blood of ancient creatures from the Creation Times. The rivers and the paths they have chosen from inland to the sea have been created by ancient snakes searching for law breakers to punish them.'

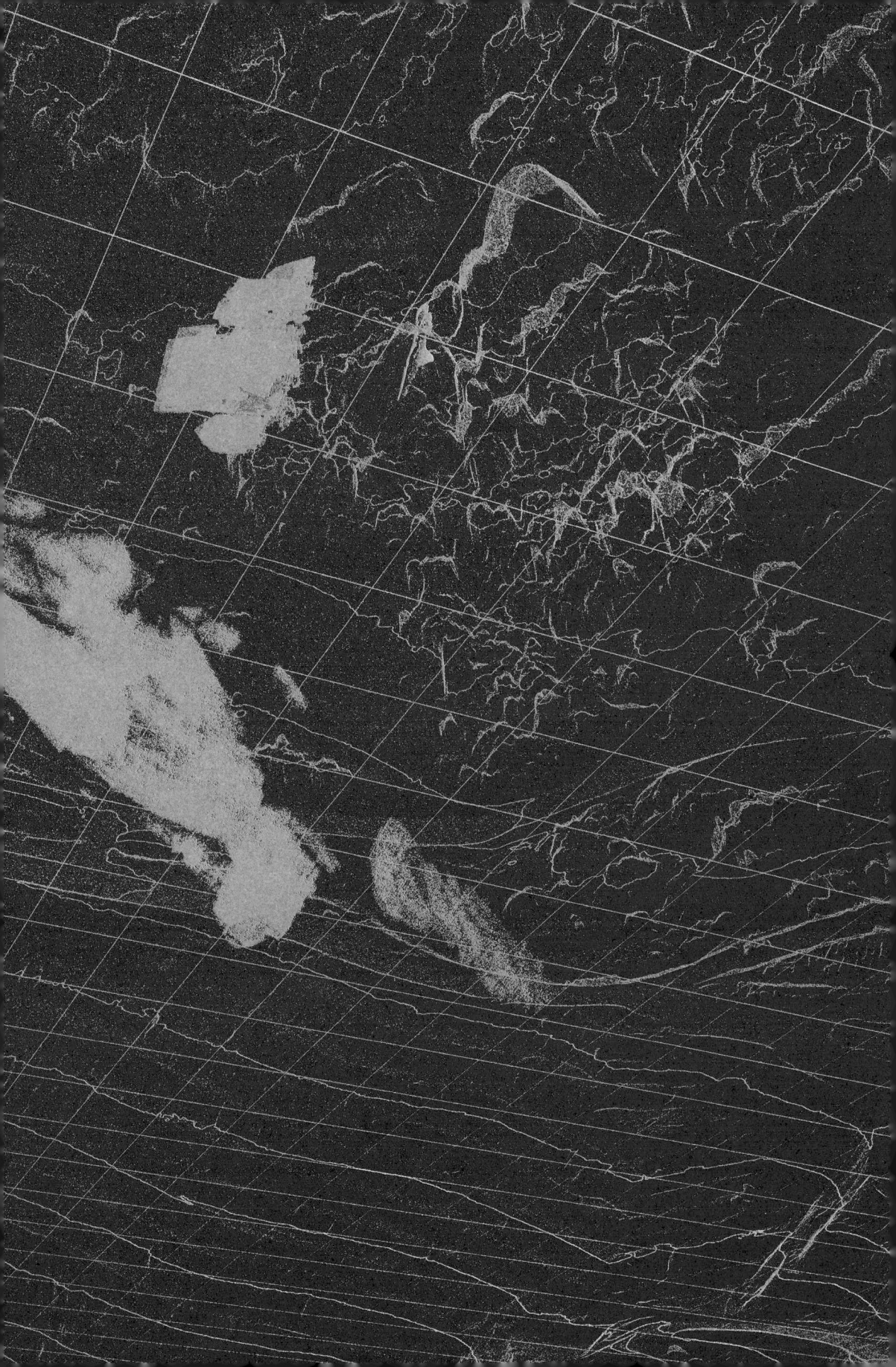

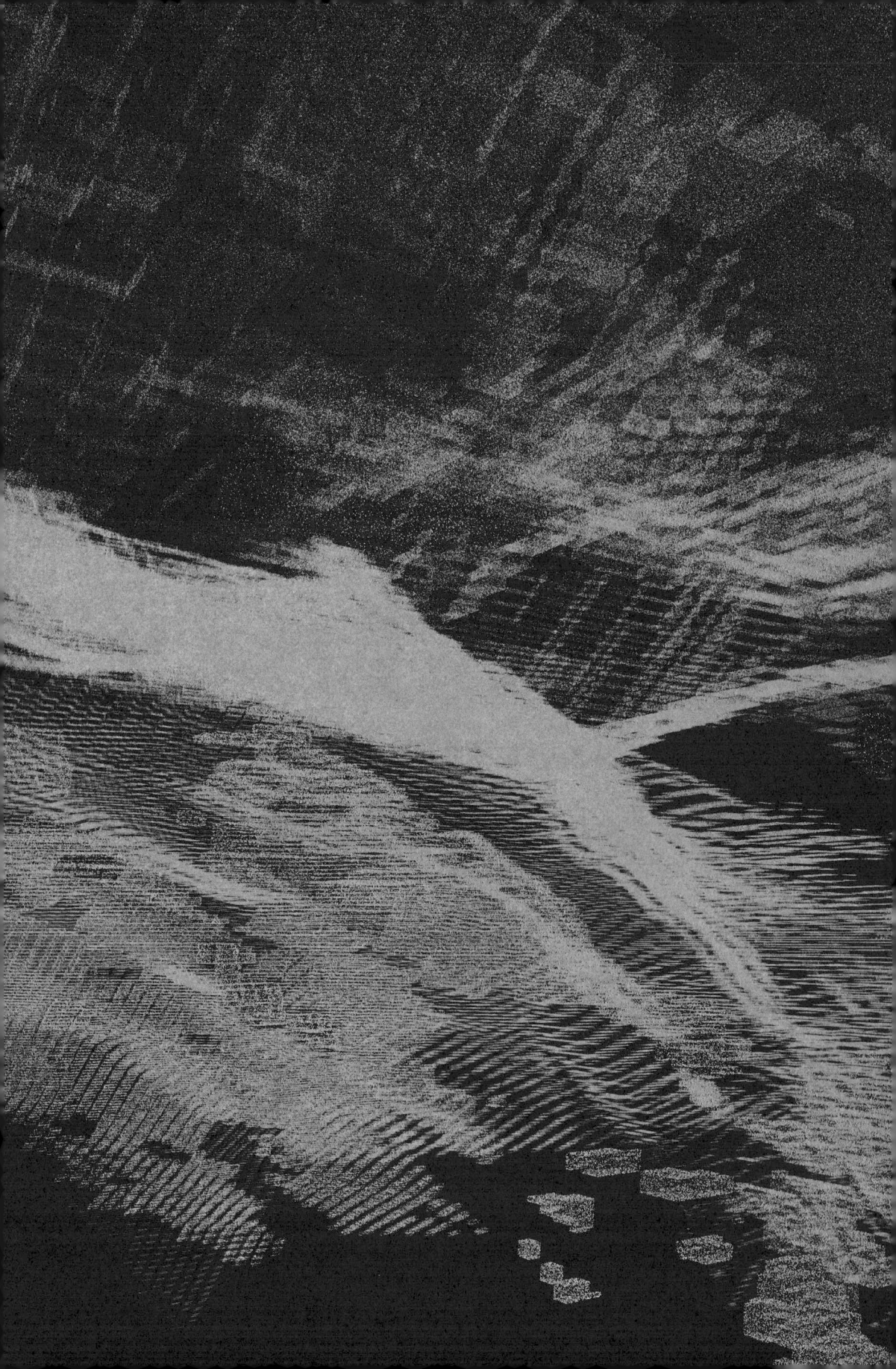

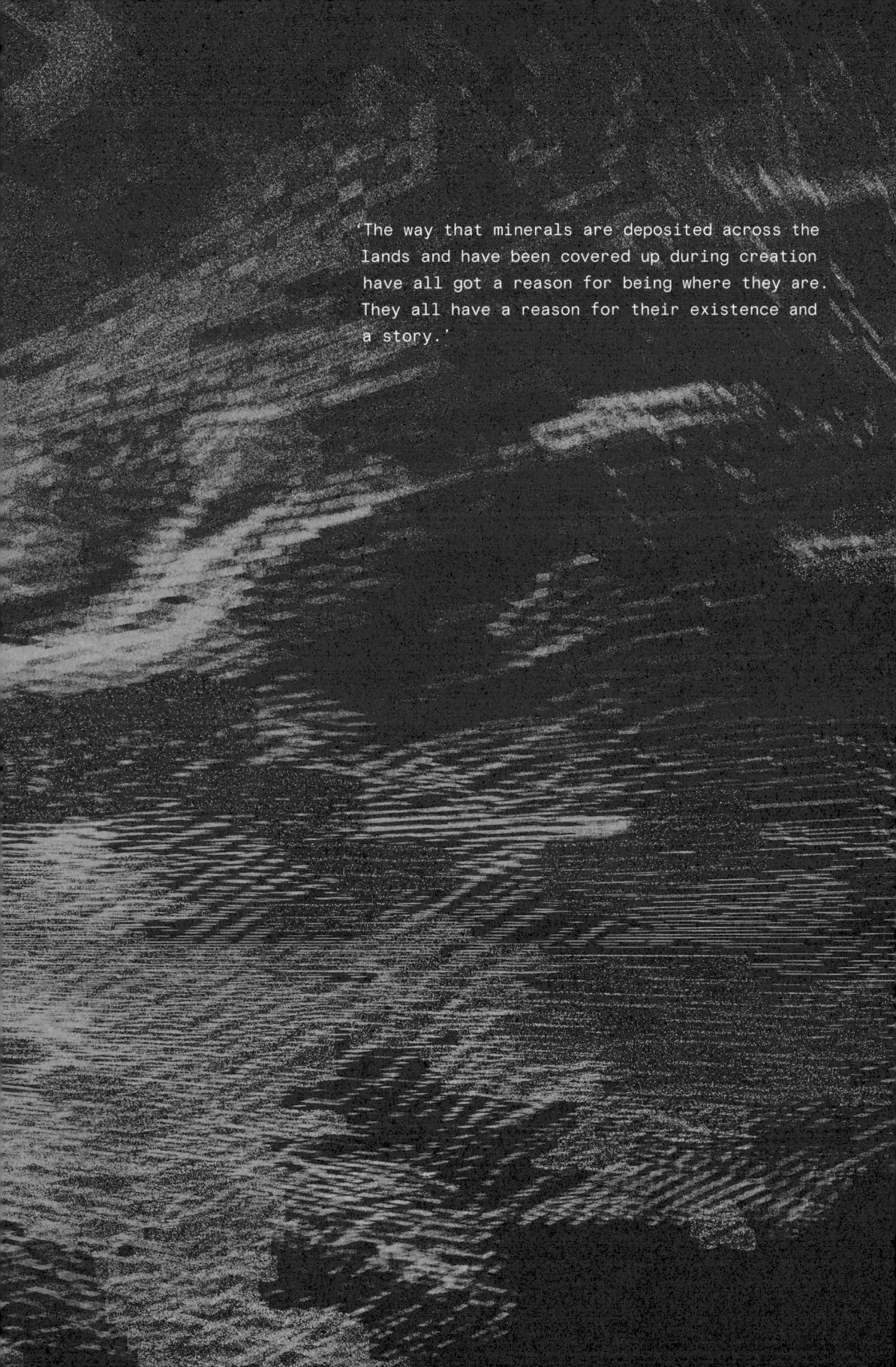

'The way that minerals are deposited across the lands and have been covered up during creation have all got a reason for being where they are. They all have a reason for their existence and a story.'

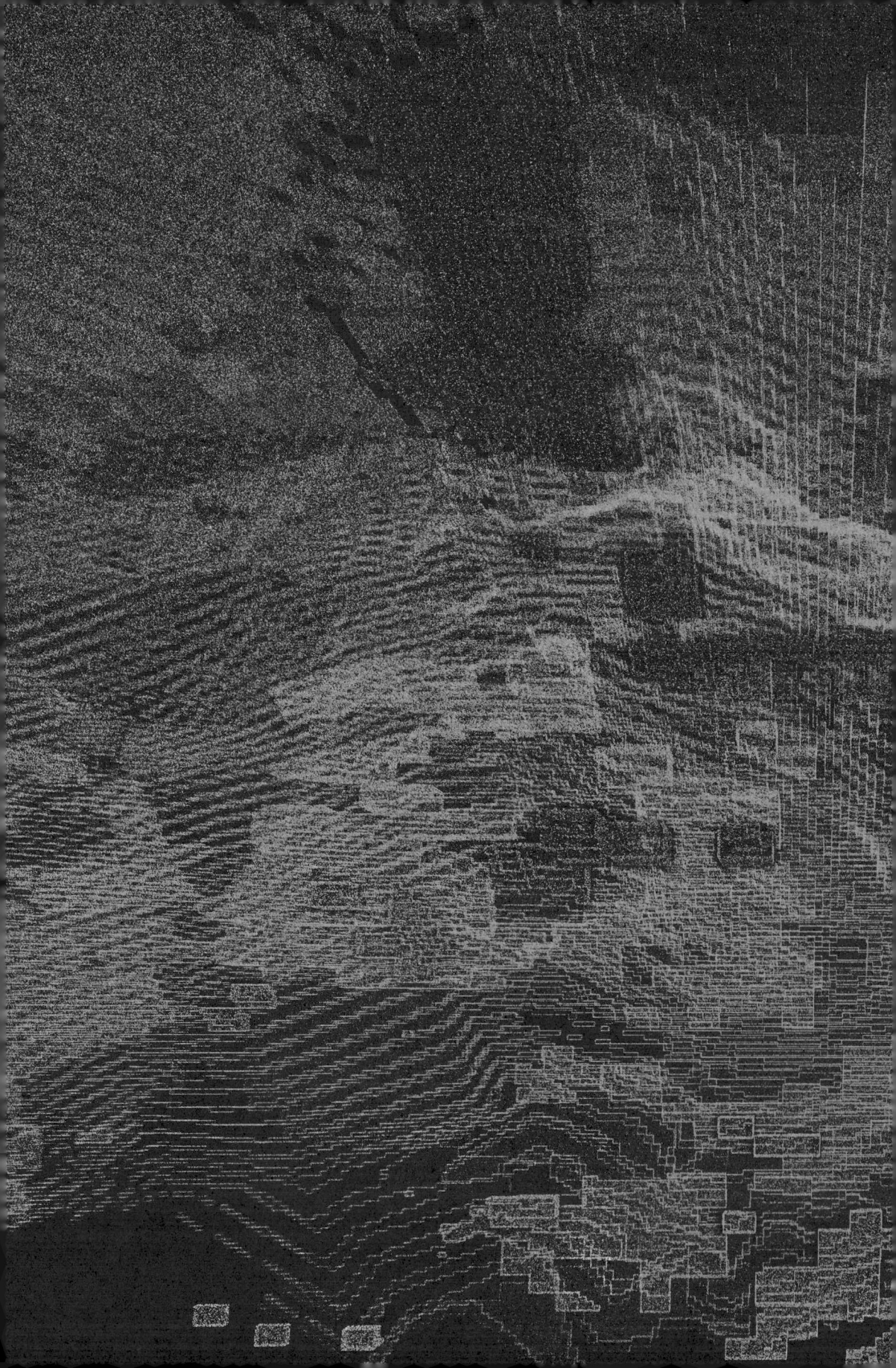

23°
39'
54.1"
S
119°
10'
56.4"
E

'Having open-cut mines and underground mines hurt the spirit of the land, she sees it, she feels it, she wonders why as she sits and cries, why are we scraping her skin, why are we taking her story?'

By Tyson Mowarin

16 g   8 g   4 g

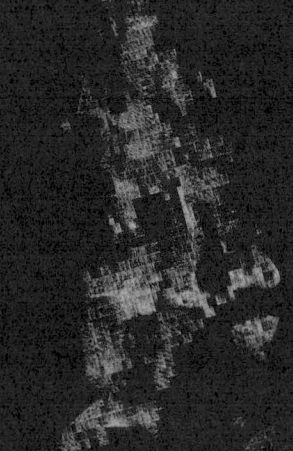

2g

One of the principle uses of gold is as an
investment instrument. A proxy for accumulated
wealth, a high stakes version of the wad of cash
under the mattress. Much of the gold extracted
from this ancient ground is done so purely so it
can be quantified and weighed. It is then shipped
across the world from one hole in the ground
to another, stored below the surface once more
in the vaults of HSBC or the federal reserve,
Here it remains, to be traded virtually. The
gold price is a culturally constructed value,
a financial fiction, embodied in a block of
material which has been wrung like blood from
a stone – two grams from a tonne of earth on
average. In the cool calculations of the digital
mine model, the shape of the excavation changes
as the variable gold price is entered into the
software. As the gold price rises it becomes
more economical to mine areas of lower gold
ore concentration. The model reveals the various
grades of a single gold ore-body in grams per
tonne and as the price drops the virtual mine
shrinks as the software focuses around deposits
of richer gold ore. One cut at a time, the
fluctuations of the gold price are etched into
the ground of Western Australia, forging deep
underground caverns and open pit excavations
the scale of the Grand Canyon. That steamy black
void in which Unknown Fields stood is a live
graph, shaped by the frequency of electronic
trades in London and New York and from such
distances we can so dramatically affect a
landscape that doesn't belong to us.

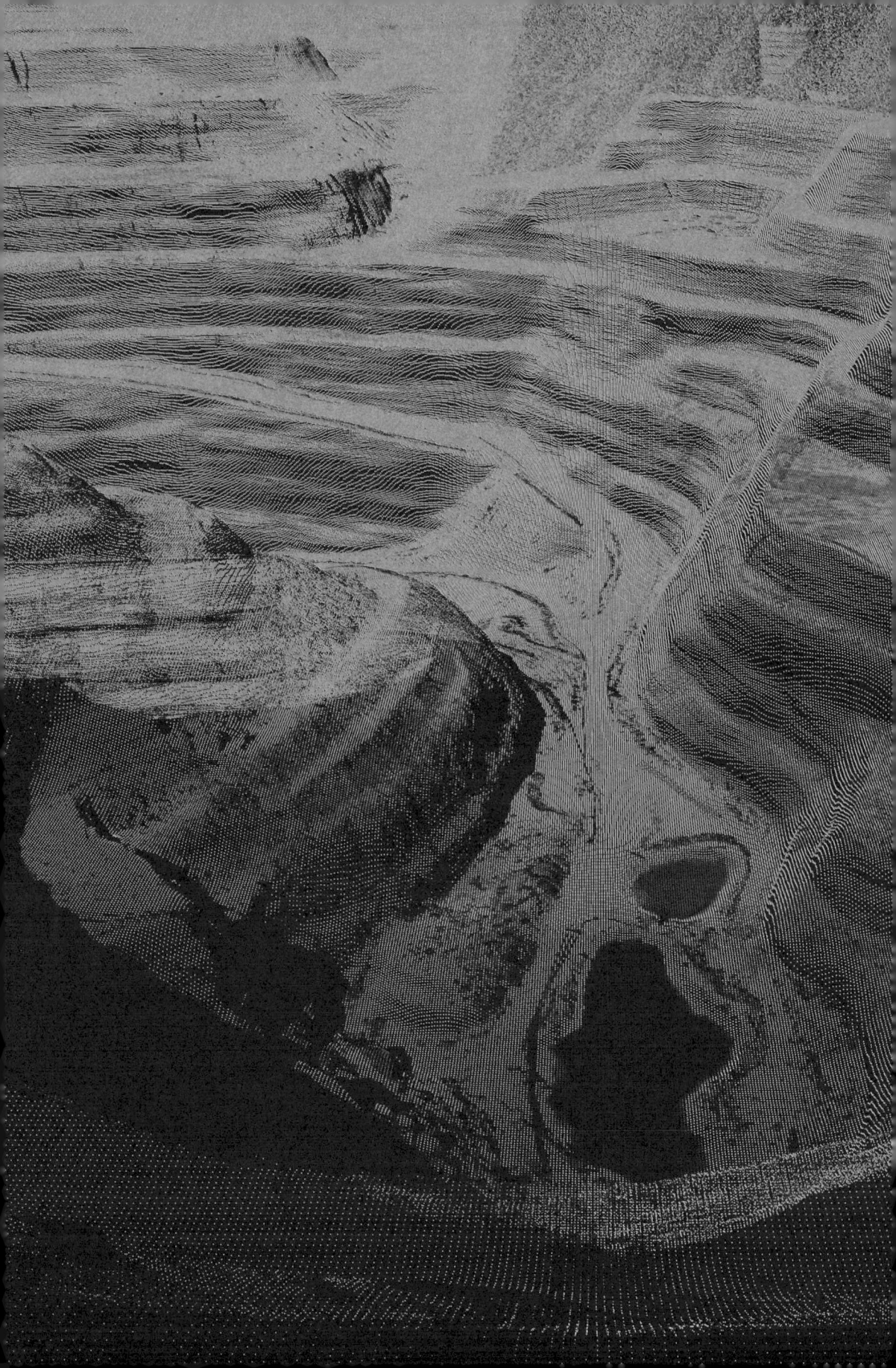

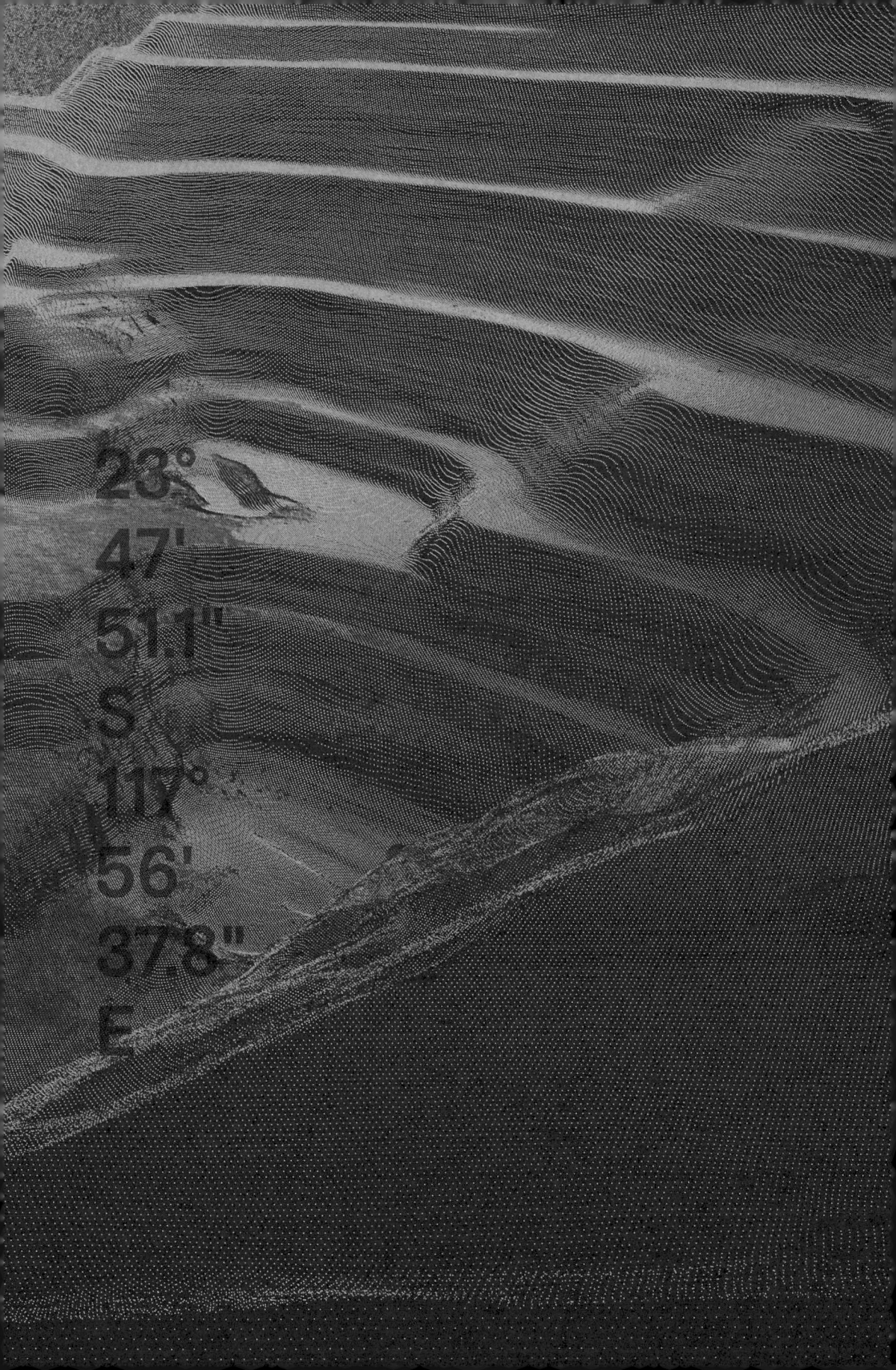

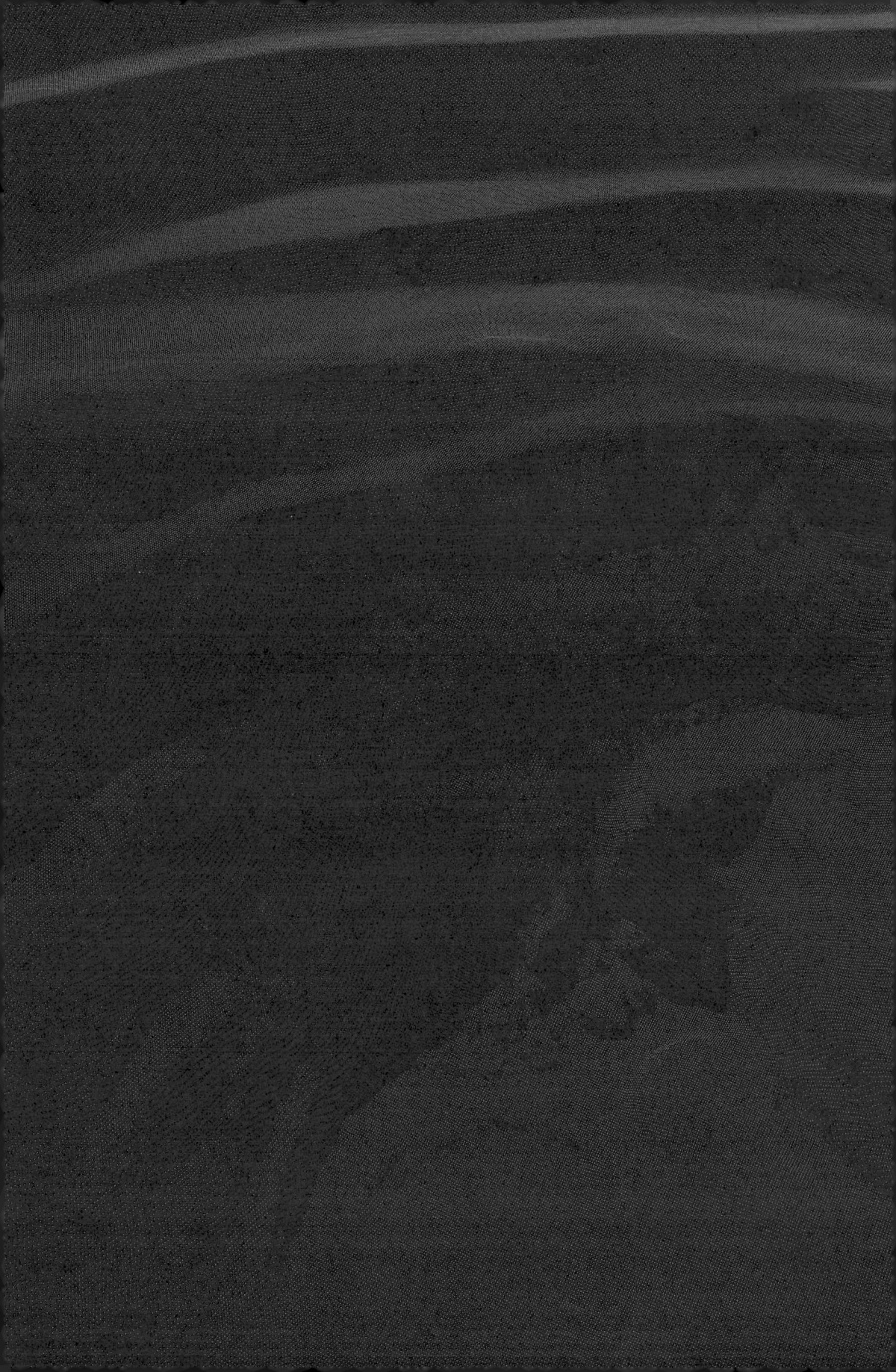

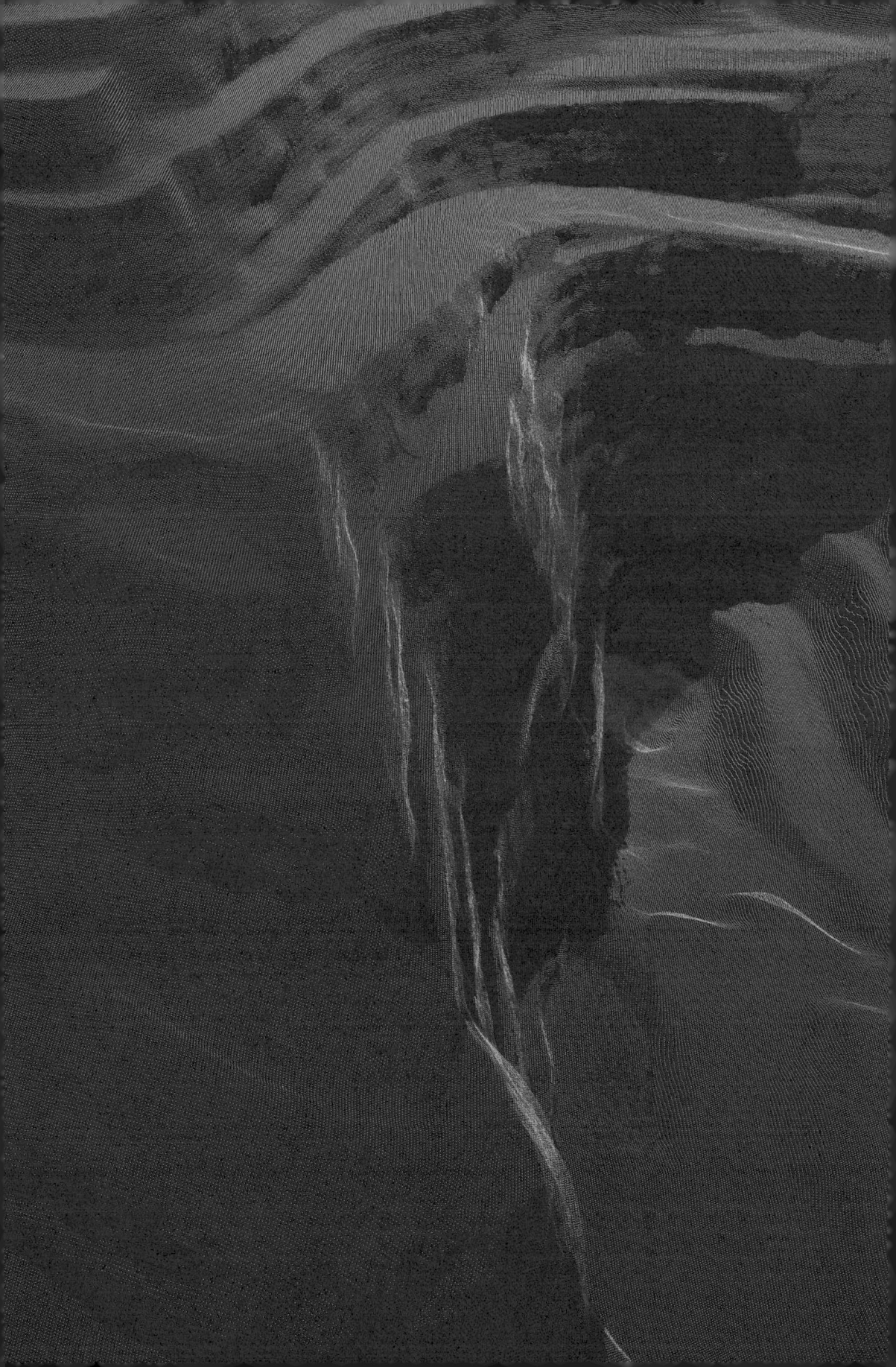

All Mine

Unknown Fields have built a domestic mining machine with a data connection to the precious metals market. A numbers game that carves mountains across the other side of the world is brought home to live with us in more familiar territories. It is live-linked to the gold price as it trades: $1302, $1320, $1314 per ounce. Tracking its percentage rise and fall, the miner carves into the everyday. The abstractions of buying and selling play out in our comfortable mundane, excavating our domestic landscapes.

The financial foundations of the lives we lead and the things we own are propped up on investment commodities and the fluctuating values assigned to them. This abstract stream of numbers and the distant landscapes they carve are both obscure alien realms. You sit at your kitchen table, it mines, the price rises, your world is excavated as you sip your coffee as you read the morning papers. It mines as you sleep, as you take a bath, as you watch TV. What was once out of sight, lost to distance, just a sacrificial territory in a place we will never visit is now bought home, screeching and drilling into the cities and spaces we all know so well.

    The landscape of Australia is both everywhere and nowhere. Here in the red ochre of the Never Never we are carving our desires into the archaeological record, a new creation story for our endless city.

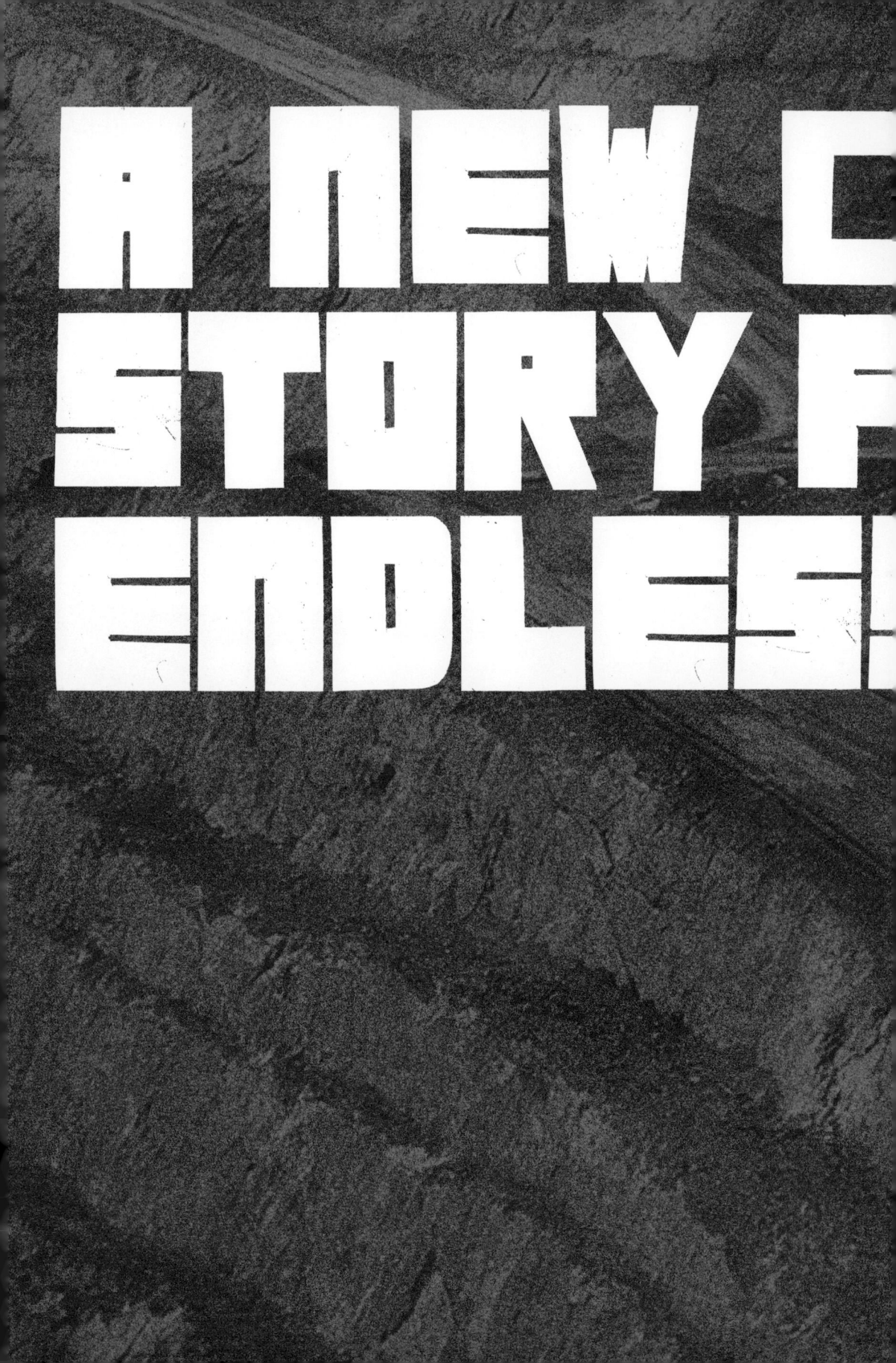

REATION
OR OUR
CITY

Never Never Lands by Unknown Fields

Design: Neasden Control Centre & City Edition Studio
Illustration: Neasden Control Centre

Printed in Italy by Musumeci
ISBN 978-1-907896-85-9

© 2016 Architectural Association and the Author

No part of this book may be reproduced in any manner whatsoever without written permission from the publisher, except in the context of reviews

For a catalogue of AA Publications visit
aaschool.ac.uk/publications or email publications@aaschool.ac.uk

AA Publications
36 Bedford Square
London
WC1B 3ES
t + 44 (0)20 7887 4021
f + 44 (0)20 7414 0783